T0276265

# A Persian Kitchen Tale

*Discover Exciting Flavors Through 60 Simple Recipes*

## Haniyeh Nikoo

PAGE STREET
PUBLISHING CO.

PAGE STREET
PUBLISHING CO.

Copyright © 2024 Haniyeh Nikoo

First published in 2024 by

Page Street Publishing Co.

27 Congress Street, Suite 1511

Salem, MA 01970

www.pagestreetpublishing.com

All rights reserved. No part of this book may be reproduced or used, in any form or by any means, electronic or mechanical, without prior permission in writing from the publisher.

Distributed by Macmillan, sales in Canada by The Canadian Manda Group.

28   27   26   25   24     1   2   3   4   5

ISBN-13: 979-8-89003-055-9

Library of Congress Control Number: 2023945020

Edited by Marissa Giambelluca

Cover and book design by Meg Baskis for Page Street Publishing Co.

Photography and food styling by Haniyeh Nikoo

Author portraits by Leandro Silva

Printed and bound in China

Page Street Publishing protects our planet by donating to nonprofits like The Trustees, which focuses on local land conservation.

For Noora:

Remember *home* is where your heart belongs.

# Contents

*Preface*   7

*Persian Cuisine: A Brief Introduction*   10

*Special Ingredients*   13

   Rice (Berenj/برنج)   13

   Buttermilk Paste (Kashk/کشک)   13

   Barberry (Zereshk/زرشک)   14

   Dried Lime (Limoo Amaani/لیموعمانی)   14

   Saffron (Zaferaan/زعفران)   16

   Persian Hogweed (Golpar/گلپر)   16

   Young Grape (Ghooreh/غوره)   17

A FEW STAPLES IN
A PERSIAN KITCHEN   19

Rice Mixed Spices
(Adviyeh Poloyi/ادویه پلویی)   21

Stew Mixed Spices
(Adviyeh Khoreshti/ادویه خورشتی)   22

Persian-Style Crispy Fried Onions
(Piyaaz Daagh/پیازداغ)   25

Mixed Herbs Chutney (Dallaar/دلار)   26

ON THE GRILL   29

Ground Beef Kabaab
(Kabaab Koobideh/کباب کوبیده)   31

Chicken Kabaab (Joojeh Kabaab/جوجه کباب)   32

Sweet & Sour Kabaab (Kabaab Torsh/کباب ترش)   35

Stuffed Fish (Maalaa Beej/مالابیج)   36

RICE & MORE   39

Persian Plain Rice (Chelo/چلو)   41

Persian Crispy Rice Three Ways (Tahdig/ته دیگ)   42

Rainbow Rice with Lamb
(Qeymeh Nesaar/قیمه نثار)   49

Mung Bean, Tahini & Date Rice
(Maash va Ardeh Polo/ماش و ارده پلو)   51

Spicy Shrimp Rice with Tamarind
(Meygoo Polo/میگو پلو)   55

Green Beans & Beef Pilaf (Loobiyaa Polo/لوبیا پلو)   57

Lentil Rice with Raisins & Ground Beef
(Adas Polo/عدس پلو)   61

Carrot Rice with Chicken Thighs
(Havij Polo/هویج پلو)   63

Saffron, Yogurt & Chicken Rice Pilaf
(Tahchin Morgh/تهچین مرغ)   67

Broad Bean & Dill Pilaf (Baaqaali Polo/باقالی پلو)   71

STEWS OF ALL KINDS   73

Herby Bean Stew with Smoked Fish
(Baaqla Qaatoq/باقلا قاتوق)   75

Walnut, Pumpkin & Pomegranate Stew
(Kadoo Fesenjan/کدو فسنجان)   76

Celery & Lamb Stew
(Khoresht-e Karafs/خورشت کرفس)   79

Eggplant, Lamb & Tomato Stew
(Khoresht-e Baademjaan/خورشت بادمجان)   80

Tamarind Spicy Fish Stew
(Qaliyeh Maahi/قلیه ماهی)   83

Braised Lamb Shank (Maahicheh/ماهیچه)   84

Chicken in Pomegranate Sauce
(Khoresht-e Naardoon/خورشت ناردون)   87

Lamb & Beans Stew (Aabgoosht/آبگوشت)   88

Meatballs in Mint & Vinegar Sauce
(Naafeleh Khoozestaani/نافله خوزستانی)   91

IN THE BOWL   93

Buttermilk, Walnut & Tomato Soup
(Kaaljoosh/کالجوش)   95

Bean & Tomato Stew
(Khoraak-e Loobiaa/خوراک لوبیا)   96

Spicy Red Lentil Daal
(Daal Adas-e Booshehri/دال عدس بوشهری)   99

Barley & Cilantro Soup (Soup-e Jo va Geshniz-e
Tabrizi/سوپ جو و گشنیز تبریزی)   100

Cold Yogurt Soup with Fresh Herbs & Nuts
(Aab-Doogh Khiyaar/آبدوغ خیار)   103

## BREAKFAST & BRUNCH — 105

Butternut Squash Patties
(Kouyi Kaakaa/کویی کاکا) — 107

Spinach Onion Omelet (Nargessi/نرگسی) — 108

Fried Cheese Omelet
(Panir Bereshteh/پنیربرشته) — 111

Tomato Paste Omelet with Beans
(Omelete Shaapoori/املت شاپوری) — 112

Date, Walnut & Sesame Omelet (Qisaavaa/قیساواو) — 115

Clotted Cream (Sarshir/سرشیر) — 116

Quince Jam (Morabbaa-ye- Beh/مربای به) — 119

## SOMETHING TO SHARE — 121

Lettuce & Dill Patties
(Kookoo Kaahoo Shevid/کوکوی کاهو شوید) — 123

Spicy Shrimp & Potatoes
(Dopiyaazeh Meygoo/دوپیازه میگو) — 124

Smoky Eggplant & Walnut Dip
(Kaal Kabaab/کال کباب) — 127

Meat & Potato Patties (Kotlet/کتلت) — 128

Tabrizi Stuffed Eggplant
(Gaarni Yaarikh/گارنی یاریخ) — 131

Smoky Eggplant & Tomato Spread
(Mirzaa Qaasemi/میرزا قاسمی) — 132

Eggplant & Buttermilk Spread
(Kashk-e Baademjaan/کشک بادمجان) — 135

## SOMETHING TO APPETIZE — 137

Roasted Eggplant & Yogurt Dip
(Boraani Baademjaan/بورانی بادمجان) — 139

Spinach & Yogurt Dip
(Boraani Esfenaaj/بورانی اسفناج) — 140

Yogurt & Cucumber Dip
(Maast va Khiyaar/ماست و خیار) — 143

Marinated Olives with Herbs, Pomegranate &
Walnuts (Zeytoon Parvardeh/زیتون پرورده) — 144

Quick Pickled Smoky Eggplant & Herbs
(Naaz Khaatoon/ناز خاتون) — 147

Quick Mango Pickle (Torshi Anbeh/ترشی انبه) — 148

Shirazi Salad (سالاد شیرازی) — 151

## SOMETHING SWEET — 153

Milk Halva (Halvaa-ye Shir/حلوای شیر) — 155

Ginger Halva (Halvaa-ye Zanjebil/حلوای زنجبیل) — 156

Deep-Fried Mini Buns with Nuts & Spices
(Qottaab/قطاب) — 159

Sesame Sweet Bread (Naan-e Komaaj/نان کماج) — 160

Date & Nuts Mini Pies (Kolompeh/کلمپه) — 163

Rice Vermicelli & Rose Water Granita
(Faaloodeh/فالوده) — 164

Saffron & Cardamom Buns
(Naan-e Shirmaal Zaferaani/نان شیرمال زعفرانی) — 167

*Acknowledgments* — *169*

*About the Author* — *171*

*Index* — *172*

# PREFACE

Thirty-two years ago, I was nine years old living in a tiny apartment in Tehran with my parents and two younger siblings. My favorite activity then was reading. I would read anything I could get my hands on: old newspapers, novels and classical poetry, a combination of things I did and did not understand. To satiate my thirst for reading, my mom began to buy me more age-appropriate books. One of these books explained the old Persian sayings and proverbs in the form of stories. There was a story that talked about making the perfect *chelo*, a classic Persian steamed rice dish, and taught that there is no shame in asking for help if you do not know how to do something. The story lacked the precision of measurements and methods found in a cookbook, but I used it to cook rice while my mother was away.

When she returned, I ran to the door and proudly told her that I cooked my very own chelo without her. Her eyes widened with suspicion, but after trying my dish, she admitted that I did well. This had been my first time cooking alone, and the Persian story was my first introduction to the concept of a cookbook. Many years have passed, and I have cooked countless dishes, but one thing has stuck with me since then: cooking intuitively.

Growing up, I was not particularly adventurous with food. I remember clearly disliking certain tastes, textures or dishes, even into my early adulthood. But I was curious about how to do things and always wanted to find the answers myself. This attitude led me to cook that first batch of rice and continues with me in the kitchen today.

My brother and I always competed over who was a better cook. We had our own ways of baking, cooking and trying to please our audience of parents and family members. He found his path early and grew up to become a chef with his own restaurant. My passion for reading, writing and art took me in a different direction.

Fast forward to 2009. I left my country for the first time to continue my higher education in visual arts at the University of Strasbourg in France. I remained a passionate cook, and I was excited to start trying different cuisines. I remember the joy of my first taste of sushi and my first Indian feast; in my kitchen, I traveled the world—from France to Italy, China, Vietnam, Lebanon and more.

Amidst all these delightful new experiences, homesickness was creeping in. No matter how much I loved and appreciated the new adventurous life I had found living alone abroad, I couldn't shake the longing for the familiar smells, sounds and tastes of home: the scent of the air, the trees, the street foods, hearing the murmur of my native language on the bus and streets and in stores. I was missing my home.

Out of all the experiences I was longing for, food was the one I could bring back to my life. Persian food and holidays (and the friends that came with them) became a tether connecting me to my homeland and eased the pain of distance.

Since Strasbourg, life has taken me to six different countries or cities, and I held on to the tether of Persian cooking, poetry and music to stay connected to my roots. During all my international moves, I have carried my home in little jars of spices. I always packed the kitchen last and unpacked it first once we arrived at the new home. No matter where I lived, while still curious about new foods and cultures, I filled my own home with familiar aromas and tastes.

This book is a journey that has come full circle. Starting with my first pot of chelo 32 years ago, I have had a long and winding path of creative discovery. Beyond cooking, I've enjoyed a lifelong passion for writing, painting and poetry. Studying the visual arts led to learning photography. In 2018 I started taking pictures of the meals I was cooking; soon after I began my Instagram page as a food photographer. As time passed and people began asking for my recipes, I learned to tame my desire to cook intuitively with the need for structure and measurement. Throughout the years, I've come to understand how to utilize my writing, storytelling and visual presentation skills in order to share recipes with my audience in an inviting manner.

When the opportunity to write a cookbook arose, I had no doubt that it should be about Persian cuisine. This wasn't just about me being Iranian—I believe the country's political climate has isolated this rich and flavorful cuisine from the rest of the world. While several excellent Persian cookbooks are already available, our national cuisine still has a way to go regarding global recognition.

Thanks to social media, there has been a surge of interest in diverse cultures and cuisines. Authentic dishes from all over the world can now be shared with others in mere seconds. This has led us to encounter and crave foods from faraway places we have yet to visit and try to recreate them in the comfort of our own homes. Iran is slowly joining this blooming globalized kitchen.

The day I returned to Berlin from my trip to Tehran in 2022, the "Woman, Life, Freedom" movement blossomed. I wrote the recipes for this book, cooked them and photographed them as my mind was occupied, and my heart was aching with the news of this unfolding movement. With pride as an Iranian, I dedicate this book to all the brave women of my country, those who took the pain of leaving and those who stayed, fearlessly fighting for their rights, for "Woman, Life, Freedom."

# PERSIAN CUISINE:
## A BRIEF INTRODUCTION

Every cuisine tells a rich history narrated by aromas and flavors. Persian cuisine is one of the oldest and most influential in the world. With the Silk Road running through modern Iran, Persian cuisine has had interchangeable influence with the culinary traditions of Central Asia, Greece, the Caucasus, the Levant and Turkey. Additionally, the Persian culinary style, beginning in the twelfth century, significantly impacted the rich culinary traditions of the Indian subcontinent.

Over the centuries, Iranian cuisine has developed numerous regional culinary traditions, each boasting its own unique flavor profile, which includes Caspian, Azerbaijani, Kurdish and southern Iranian cuisines.

In Iran, traditional meals usually consist of rice, some kind of meat, vegetables and herbs. Regardless of the region, herbs are always a prominent component of the cuisine. Using herbs to add flavor to a dish means using spices in moderation. As a result, Persian cuisine is generally considered to be mild in terms of spice, except for dishes from the southern regions, which tend to be spicier. Onions are a dominant ingredient in almost every dish. Dairy products are also prominent in each meal. Cheese, yogurt and dairy drinks are used for cooking, for garnishing or as a side in abundance.

Nuts like pistachios and walnuts and fruits such as plums, pomegranates, quince, prunes, apricots and raisins are commonly used in Persian cuisine. Typical Iranian spices and seasonings include saffron, cinnamon, turmeric, cardamom, Persian hogweed (*golpar*), rose water, dried roses, barberries, dried lime, verjuice, young grapes (*ghooreh*) and tamarind.

Bread and rice are the two main staples in Iran. For centuries rice was considered the food of the wealthy and bread was considered to be for the poor. Today, both are equally valued and enjoyed in every household. Most Persian meals are meant to be served with one of these staples.

In Iranian culture, a traditional table setting is placing a tablecloth called a *sofreh* over a rug or table. The main dishes are positioned in the center and surrounded by smaller appetizers, condiments and side dishes in shared portions. At the sofreh, individuals serve themselves according to their liking. This is done out of respect for each person's unique taste and desire to control the amount of each food they like to have. However, at a Persian table, guests are served the best part of each meal and are often asked to try everything and have more. This is done to help break the ice and overcome any shyness about serving themselves. In Iranian culture, guests have a special place, and serving them the best food is one way to show hospitality and respect.

This book is an introduction to Persian cuisine for those in the West who are curious to try it without being overwhelmed by challenging techniques or ingredients that are difficult to source. My goal is for this cookbook to serve as a gateway to the rich and diverse flavors of Persian cuisine for more people.

I gathered a wide range of recipes with attention to diversity in taste, ingredients and diets. I skipped some beloved recipes I wished were in this book solely because they need some specific seasonal ingredients that can be challenging to find or have a lengthy and elaborate preparation method. My goal was to keep this selection diverse and achievable by using ingredients that are easy to find no matter where you live.

When I was younger, I wondered why so many cookbooks featured similar traditional recipes. As I began to cook seriously and write down recipes, I realized that using the same ingredients with slightly different measurements or methods could create dishes that looked similar but tasted unique. This is the beauty of cooking!

I invite you to sit at my Persian table and try these recipes as they are described and then make them your own; use less cilantro or add more garlic to your heart's content. Enjoy cooking Persian as the host of your own table.

رزق ما آید به پای میهمان از خوان غیب
میزبان ماست هر کس می‌شود مهمان ما
صائب تبریزی

*With guest's approach descends our feast from Heaven, blessed*

*Our host, therefore, is none but he who is our guest*

*Sáeb Tabrizi*

# SPECIAL INGREDIENTS

In this chapter, I will go over some unique ingredients frequently used in Persian cuisine. I have narrowed down the list to include only those ingredients that regularly appear in this book's recipes. I have also provided a readily available substitute for each item in case you have trouble finding them. However, depending on where you live, most of these ingredients are available in Middle Eastern stores or online shops.

## Rice (Berenj/برنج)

Rice plays a vital role in Persian cuisine, much like in numerous East and Central Asian cultures. The primary source of the country's rice supply comes from the northern provinces, which are blessed with a favorable climate conducive to rice cultivation.

Iranians have a strong sense of pride when it comes to their rice production and cooking techniques. The country cultivates a few distinct varieties of rice, which are renowned for their fragrant scent, extended grains, low starch content and delectable flavor.

It can be challenging to find Persian rice outside of Iran. As a result, many Iranian diasporas have opted to use Indian or Pakistani basmati rice as a replacement when cooking rice dishes. Although basmati rice may not be as fragrant as Persian rice, its long grains and less starchy texture make it a suitable alternative.

The ultimate goal when cooking rice is to have each grain separate and long. To achieve this, the rice should be cooked in hot water, drained of the starchy water and then steamed at a low temperature until cooked.

In Iran, making sticky rice is not very common. However, in the northern provinces, there is a more straightforward method of cooking white rice that can result in slightly sticky rice. This method is known as *kateh* and involves cooking rice in water with salt and no oil until the water is fully absorbed. Afterward, the rice is steamed over low heat until the grains are cooked.

This book features stew recipes that pair well with white rice, although you are welcome to use any type of rice you like. If you want to make a traditional Persian rice dish, it is recommended to choose Indian or Pakistani basmati rice. To get the best results, make sure to select long uniform grains that are slightly transparent and have a light yellow color.

## Buttermilk Paste (Kashk/کشک)

*Kashk* is a fermented dairy ingredient that is commonly used in Iranian cuisine as well as in Turkish and Greek dishes. It has a unique sour and savory flavor due to the fermentation process and is an excellent source of protein and probiotics.

Various regions have their own distinct methods of making kashk. The traditional Persian version involves draining and drying *doogh*, which is the liquid that remains after straining yogurt or buttering cream.

Modern kashk is made of drained buttermilk. The paste from draining buttermilk is shaped into balls and then dried for a longer shelf life. When needed, the dried balls are soaked in water and turned into a paste again. Nowadays, pasteurized fresh and dried kashk are made in factories and sold in jars or bags. It is available widely in online stores or most Middle Eastern shops in Western countries.

Kashk's umami flavor can be an acquired taste, but don't let this deter you from creating dishes with kashk as the primary ingredient. If you prefer a milder flavor, you can use less of it. I have also created a substitute for kashk that is milder in taste and can be found more easily in regular grocery stores. It is made by blending fresh goat cheese and buttermilk into a paste. The tangier the cheese, the better. The precise amount of this substitute is given in all the recipes that call for kashk.

I strongly suggest trying to cook with kashk at least once to experience the taste of this ancient Middle Eastern ingredient.

## Barberry (Zereshk/زرشک)

*Zereshk*, or dried barberries, are tiny oval-shaped red berries with a sour taste from evergreen shrubs. They are popular in Persian cooking as a main ingredient to cook with or as a garnish. Dried barberries can be found in most Middle Eastern stores or online shops in Western countries. They are dried naturally with no added sugar, which makes them great to cook with as you can add as much sugar as you wish to balance the acidic taste.

If you can't find barberries, cranberries can be a suitable alternative. While they lack the unique tanginess of barberries, their acidic flavor can still serve the same purpose. In this book, whenever a recipe calls for barberries, a substitute is also provided. Keep in mind that most dried cranberries are sold sweetened, so you may need to adjust the amount of added sugar to your liking. Additionally, to mimic the texture of barberries, it's recommended to finely chop the cranberries.

## Dried Lime (Limoo Amaani/لیموعمانی)

*Limoo amaani* are small limes that are dried whole, usually in the sun. They have a citrusy, sour and umami flavor and are popular in many Middle Eastern countries such as Iraq and Oman. In Persian cuisine, they are commonly used in stews, soups and herbal teas.

They are much smaller than the limes available in the Western market because they are made of a local lime in Iran called *limoo shirazi*, which is the same size as or smaller than a walnut.

Nowadays, you can buy dried limes from online shops across Europe as well as all Middle Eastern stores.

If a recipe calls for dried limes but you don't have any on hand, you can use lime juice as a substitute. While it won't have the same fermented flavor as dried limes, it will still provide the necessary citrusy and sour taste to the dish.

## Saffron (Zaferaan/زعفران)

Saffron is the golden spice that not only gets its name for the beautiful bright yellow color it adds to the dishes but is also known as the most expensive spice in the world. The high price is due to the intense labor required to harvest it.

Each strand of saffron is one thread (stigma and style) of one crocus flower. Each flower has three threads that are harvested by hand and dried. Roughly 150 flowers are needed to make 1 gram of dried saffron.

Saffron is local to the Middle East. Iran produces about 45 percent of saffron globally. Afghanistan and Spain are second and third in saffron production, respectively. Given that Iran is the main producer of saffron in the world, Iranians use it often when cooking and baking and in drinks.

Saffron not only adds a mild and pleasant flavor to the dish in addition to its golden color but also has many health benefits. Some of the studied benefits of saffron include being rich in antioxidants and having cancer-fighting properties. It can boost mood, increase libido and alleviate PMS pain. Some studies suggest it can be an effective antidepressant when consumed in small daily doses. However, it is crucial to consult your doctor before using saffron as a medicine, since incorrect dosage or daily usage can result in unwanted side effects.

Although saffron is expensive, a little bit goes a long way. I recommend finding a Middle Eastern shop in your neighborhood or online to buy high-quality saffron for a fraction of the price found in major grocery shops. Using saffron in many dishes presented in this book is optional, but I recommend using this precious ingredient if available.

Before using saffron, it is necessary to brew it. There are various methods of brewing. Some suggest adding hot water and letting it sit, while others claim that using ice cubes to brew gives better results. Alternatively, you can turn the saffron into a fine powder, add a few tablespoons (30 ml) of cold water and let it sit for 10 to 15 minutes, which is just as effective as other methods. Use the resulting red liquid in your recipe, and if there is any leftover brewed saffron, you can store it in an airtight container in the fridge for up to a week or use it in your tea.

## Persian Hogweed (Golpar/گلپر)

*Golpar* is a spice derived from the seeds of Persian hogweed. It has an aromatic quality with a slightly bitter taste. This spice is commonly used as a powder to garnish soups, stews and occasionally fruits such as pomegranate. It's believed to reduce the bloating caused by legumes, hence it is sprinkled over many legume-based dishes.

It is also used in some *adviyeh* (spice mixes) to marinate fish and chicken and to flavor rice.

Unfortunately, there is no substitute in terms of taste for this spice. In many dishes, the use of it is optional, as excluding it would have a minor effect. It's available to buy as a powder in online shops and most Middle Eastern stores.

If you are not familiar with golpar spice, it has a unique taste that may take some getting used to. I suggest using a small amount to garnish when you're first trying it out to become accustomed to the flavor.

## Young Grape (Ghooreh/غوره)

*Ghooreh* is the Persian name for the unripe grape that has an acidic flavor and is used frequently in Persian cuisine. The acidity is milder, lighter than lemon or lime, and different in taste. The seedless young grapes are used whole in some dishes to add acidity, like in the Eggplant, Lamb and Tomato Stew on page 80. The juice of the young grapes (verjuice/*Aabghooreh*/آبغوره) is also used in cooking and as dressing in salads, like the Shirazi Salad (page 151). Although verjuice is available in some Western grocery stores in the vinegar section, the fruit itself is something you can only find in the frozen section of Middle Eastern stores. If you have access to a winery, you can also harvest your own ghooreh and freeze them to use in cooking, or juice them and keep the juice in a clean bottle in the fridge for cooking and dressings.

In the recipes provided in this book, whenever ghooreh or the juice has been used as a substitute, lemon or lime juice is mentioned. Although it tastes different, it will add the acidity needed to the dish.

# A Few Staples in a Persian Kitchen

In addition to the unique ingredients covered in the previous chapter, Persian cuisine also incorporates a variety of common cooking ingredients. These include tomato paste, spices such as turmeric and cinnamon, legumes, garlic and more, which are readily available in most kitchens. However, to simplify the process of cooking Persian dishes, it is recommended to prepare certain staples in larger quantities beforehand. This eliminates the hassle of searching for and measuring each ingredient separately every time you cook. For example, adviyeh, a popular blend of spices with numerous variations, or crispy fried onions are essential ingredients in almost every Persian dish.

This chapter includes some essential recipes to simplify and speed up the cooking process for the dishes in this book.

# RICE MIXED SPICES

(Adviyeh Poloyi/ادویه پلویی)

*Adviyeh is the name for any mixed spice Iranians use for cooking. For example, curry is a kind of adviyeh made of a specific combination of spices. There are many different adviyeh to use in various dishes with fish, meat, rice and so on. In many houses, a family has their own recipe for an adviyeh passed through generations. Here I present the two most common spice mixes that are used throughout this book. Make and store them for your Persian cooking feasts.*

## YIELDS ABOUT ¾ CUP (100 G)

4 tbsp (32 g) ground cinnamon

4 tsp (8 g) ground cumin

4 tsp (8 g) ground green cardamom

8 tsp (20 g) edible rose petals (optional, see Note)

4 tsp (8 g) ground coriander

4 tsp (8 g) ground ginger

1 tsp ground cloves

1 tsp ground nutmeg

I would recommend using the whole seeds or barks of each spice and grinding them yourself, as they will be a lot more fragrant than store-bought powders. If you cannot find them whole, use the powdered version.

Combine the spices together. Store the spice mix in an airtight container.

### NOTE

Edible, fragrant rose petals shouldn't be too hard to find, as they also get used often in cocktails, but if you cannot find them, feel free to omit.

# STEW MIXED SPICES
## (Adviyeh Khoreshti/ادویه خورشتی)

*This spice mix is wonderful in stews. Some Persian stews have a specific set of spices. Here I've included the more commonly used spices. Preparing this adviyeh in advance will make cooking stews a lot easier.*

### YIELDS ABOUT ⅔ CUP (75 G)

2 tbsp (19 g) ground turmeric

2 tbsp (16 g) ground cinnamon

2 tbsp (12 g) ground cumin

2 tbsp (12 g) ground coriander

1 tbsp (7 g) paprika

1 tsp ground black pepper

1 tsp ground red pepper

I would recommend using the whole seeds or barks of each spice and grinding them yourself, as they will be a lot more fragrant than store-bought powders. If you cannot find them whole, use the powdered version.

Combine the spices together. Store the spice mix in an airtight container.

# PERSIAN-STYLE CRISPY FRIED ONIONS

(Piyaaz Daagh/پیازداغ)

*It's no secret that onions have a special place in Persian cooking. We use them abundantly, and fried onions are the base of most Persian dishes. However, using crispy onions to garnish is another way to bring this beloved vegetable to life. These thin and even strands of onions with a golden color and a perfect crisp are so delicious that they can be enjoyed as a snack. The caramelized sweetness of the onions with a dash of salt makes them ideal for topping soups, dips or rice plates.*

*Here is the Persian method of making perfect crispy onions. We usually make them in big batches and freeze them for later use.*

### YIELDS 1 CUP (50 G)

1 tbsp (18 g) salt

3½ cups (400 g) yellow or white onions, halved and thinly sliced

1½–2 cups (330–440 ml) cooking oil

In a pot, bring 3¼ cups (750 ml) of water to a boil and add the salt. Cook the sliced onions in the boiling water for about 5 minutes. Drain the onions and lay them flat on a paper towel.

Add the cooking oil to a small deep pot and heat over medium heat. Then add the onions in three to four batches. Watch them closely and stir occasionally for even cooking—once they start changing color, the onions can quickly become burnt. Once the onions turn lightly golden, remove them from the pot using a slotted spoon. Lay them in a dish lined with a paper towel.

Repeat with the remaining batches of onions. Once cooled, you can store the fried onions in the fridge for about 2 weeks or freeze them.

# MIXED HERBS CHUTNEY

## (Dallaar/دلار)

*This salty green paste, also known as green salt, is made with a mix of salt and wild herbs from the north of Iran. It is used in salads or as a seasoning in some dishes. Because of the amount of salt used, the chutney will last longer in the fridge, and having a jar in the refrigerator is always handy.*

*I have fond memories of a relative making traditional chutney, sitting in the little yard of her house in Rasht. My eyes were pinned at her hands, rubbing all the herbs and salt with a heavy river stone in a big clay tray until it came together into a fragrant green paste. It was therapeutic! Then she would hand me a spoonful and I would dip my cucumber in it. A match made in heaven.*

### YIELDS ABOUT 2 CUPS (492 G)

3½ cups (210 g) chopped cilantro

¾ cup (70 g) chopped mint

⅔ cup (35 g) oregano

2½ tbsp (45 g) salt

Combine the cilantro, mint and oregano in a bowl with the salt. Process the mixture through your food processor until the texture becomes softer and slightly paste-like.

Use a small amount of Mixed Herbs Chutney in your salad dressing. I also like to use it in my fruit salads—you'll be surprised how beautifully this herby and salty paste pairs with sweet and sour fruits.

Store the chutney in an airtight jar in the fridge. To prevent spoiling, use a clean spoon when taking the chutney out of the jar. This chutney can last up to 6 months with no visual spoiling.

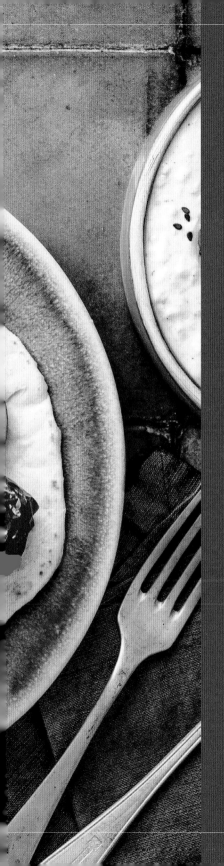

# On the Grill

*Kabaabs are an inseparable part of Persian cuisine. A delicious meat dish that originates in the Middle Eastern and Central Asian cuisines, kabaabs have many variations that are now popular all over the world. Kabaabs typically consist of cut-up or ground meat, sometimes with vegetables and other accompaniments, arranged on a skewer and grilled on charcoal. While lamb is traditionally used, regional variations may include beef, goat, chicken or fish.*

*There are numerous recipes for kabaab, each using different marinades. In this chapter, I've gathered four recipes featuring ground beef, chicken, lamb and fish.*

# GROUND BEEF KABAAB

(Kabaab Koobideh/کباب کوبیده)

*No matter where you go in Iran, kabaab koobideh is loved all over the country. While koobideh has many recipes, the differences are in the details. Given how well loved this dish is, it's a good recipe for chefs to show off how they can make it more tender or flavorful than their peers. In the end, a good koobideh must be tender, juicy and well seasoned.*

## SERVES 3–4

1¼ cups (200 g) finely grated yellow onions

¼ tsp baking soda (optional, see Note)

1.1 lb (500 g) ground beef (higher fat percentage) or a mix of lamb and beef

1 tsp salt

½ tsp ground black pepper

½ tsp paprika

A dash of powdered saffron (optional)

2 tbsp (30 ml) cold water (optional)

4 tomatoes

7 oz (200 g) sweet Italian green peppers

2 tbsp (28 g) butter (optional)

Roasted veggies, to serve

Persian Plain Rice (page 41) or flatbread, to serve

In a bowl, combine the onions and baking soda (if using), then mix in the ground beef. Add the salt, pepper and paprika and massage the meat for 2 to 3 minutes, until well combined.

If using the saffron, add it to a ramekin with the cold water and mix, then set aside.

Cut the tomatoes in half if using large tomatoes. Using the oven or a grill, roast the tomatoes and green peppers until slightly charred.

You can make the kabaab on the grill, on the stove in a grill pan or in an air fryer. I like using the grill and air fryer the best.

Shape the meat mixture into 8-inch (20-cm)-long cylinders. Flatten the cylinders slightly, then create shallow dents along the length with your finger.

If using a grill or grill pan, grill the kabaabs until browned and well-done on both sides. Refrain from overcooking, as they can get dry.

If using an air fryer, preheat to 410°F (210°C) for 5 minutes. Using the rack insert for the air fryer, lay the kabaabs in a single row without overlapping. Cook for 7 to 8 minutes, then turn them over and cook for another 3 to 4 minutes, until golden.

Melt the butter, if using, then if you've made the brewed saffron, add it to the melted butter. Once the kabaabs have finished cooking, immediately brush them with the melted butter. Serve with the roasted veggies and white rice or flatbread.

### NOTE
Adding baking soda can make the meat more tender and juicier, but it can be omitted.

# CHICKEN KABAAB
## (Joojeh Kabaab/کباب جوجه)

*Iranians love kabaab in all forms. Joojeh kabaab is a grilled dish made with marinated young chicken meat (joojeh), but nowadays it is mainly made with chicken pieces. Like many other recipes, there are a few versions of joojeh kabaab going from north to south, west to east of Iran, but this version is commonly cooked all over the country and in many restaurants.*

### SERVES 4

⅛ tsp powdered saffron

2½ lb (1.2 kg) skinless and boneless chicken thighs or breast, cut into 2" (5-cm) chunks

2 green bell peppers, divided

3 tbsp (40 ml) olive oil

½ tsp ground black pepper

1 tsp paprika

½ tsp garlic powder

½ tsp ground thyme

2 tsp (12 g) salt

Juice of 2 lemons

2 large yellow onions, halved and thinly sliced

1 red bell pepper

14 oz (400 g) tomatoes

Persian Plain Rice (page 41) or flatbread, to serve

1 cup (24 g) basil, cilantro and green onion, to garnish (optional)

In a small ramekin, combine the saffron and ¼ cup (60 ml) cold water and set aside for 10 minutes. Then in a large mixing bowl, massage the brewed saffron into the chicken pieces until everything is coated. Set aside for 10 minutes to marinate.

Meanwhile, chop one of the green bell peppers into 1-inch (2.5-cm) chunks. Pour the olive oil into the bowl with the saffron-covered chicken pieces, and mix well. Then sprinkle in the black pepper, paprika, garlic powder, thyme and salt, and combine, coating the chicken pieces evenly. Add the lemon juice, onions and chopped green bell pepper to the bowl, and mix well. Cover the bowl, and let everything marinate in the fridge for at least 2 hours or, ideally, overnight.

Cut the remaining green bell pepper and red bell pepper into 1 to 2–inch (2.5 to 5–cm) chunks. Start building the skewers, alternating between the chicken and bell peppers. Keep the chicken thigh pieces on the same skewer, separating them from the breast pieces. The breast pieces cook faster and can get dry if cooked with the thighs. Discard any remaining marinade.

You can cook the skewers on the grill, in an air fryer or on a grill pan on the stove. Cook the kabaabs until the chicken pieces are golden and the inside is not pink. Add the tomatoes on the side of your grill, air fryer pan or grill pan to get them slightly charred.

Serve the skewers and tomatoes with white rice or flatbread. Garnish with fresh herbs like basil, cilantro or green onion if desired.

> NOTE
>
> If cooking in an air fryer, cook the skewers for about 10 minutes at 410°F (210°C), turning them over halfway through the cook time. Check for doneness and cook for another 2 minutes if needed.

# SWEET & SOUR KABAAB
(Kabaab Torsh/کباب ترش)

*Kabaab Torsh is another special recipe from the northern provinces by the Caspian Sea. Kabaab made from the tenderloin or sirloin part of beef or lamb is one of the most famous Persian foods. However, there are many ways of marinating the meat. Each region uses its local herbs and spices for the marination. I chose the kabaab torsh from the north of Iran for this book because of its unique flavors and ingredients.*

## SERVES 4

1.3 lb (600 g) beef or lamb meat (tenderloin or sirloin are best), cut into 2" (5-cm) chunks

⅓ cup (100 g) pomegranate molasses

2 yellow onions, finely chopped

⅓ cup (20 g) parsley, finely chopped

2 tbsp (10 g) mint, finely chopped

1 cup (160 g) walnuts, finely chopped

½ tsp ground black pepper

3 tbsp (50 ml) olive oil

Juice of 2 limes

Salt, as needed

4 tomatoes (optional)

1 cup (24 g) fresh herbs, such as basil and parsley, to garnish (optional)

Persian Plain Rice (page 41) or flatbread, to serve

Place the meat in a large bowl, then pour in the pomegranate molasses and massage it into the meat. Add the onions, parsley, mint and walnuts to the bowl and mix well. Then add the black pepper and olive oil and mix well. Let the kabaab mixture marinate in the fridge for at least 2 to 3 hours, ideally overnight.

After marinating, add the lime juice to the kabaab mixture and mix well. Let it come to room temperature, about 30 minutes.

Put the meat and onion pieces on four skewers, rubbing a little of the marinade off, then sprinkle with salt. Discard any remaining marinade.

If using a charcoal grill (I would recommend this method), cook the kaababs until perfectly seared and slightly browned. You can serve this kaabab well-done or medium well (just like a steak) to your liking. Alternatively, you can cook the skewers in an air fryer at 410°F (210°C) for about 6 minutes, then turn them over and cook for another 3 to 4 minutes.

Roast or grill the tomatoes to go on the side if desired. Garnish with fresh herbs and serve with white rice or flatbread.

# STUFFED FISH
(Maalaa Beej/مالابيج)

*Fish is a popular dish both in north Iran by the Caspian Sea and in southern states by the Persian Gulf. However, the cooking methods and flavor palates are different. In the north, the fish is made mostly salty, with subtly sweet, sour and herby flavors. In the south, spices are used in abundance, creating rich, spicy dishes. Maalaa Beej is a stuffed fish recipe from the north, where white fish is popular.*

SERVES 2–3

2.2 lb (1 kg) whole white fish (tilapia, seabass and haddock are good choices)

Juice of 2 limes, divided

Salt, as needed

1 tsp ground cumin

2 tsp (3 g) ground thyme

1 tsp smoked or regular paprika

2 tsp (4 g) mild curry powder

1 tsp ground coriander

½ tsp ground black pepper

½ tsp garlic powder

⅔ cup (40 g) parsley, finely chopped, divided

Cooking oil, as needed

⅔ cup (100 g) yellow onion, finely chopped

3 tbsp (20 g) walnuts

1¼ cups (20 g) cilantro, finely chopped

8 cloves garlic, finely chopped

2 tbsp (30 g) pomegranate molasses

½ cup (87 g) pomegranate arils (optional)

Wash the fish, then open the belly from the head to the tail, creating room for stuffing. If the fish is not already clean, remove all the internal organs. Pat the fish dry, then rub the inside and outside with the juice from 1 lime and salt, then set aside.

Prepare the grill or heat the oven to 428°F (220°C).

Mix the cumin, thyme, paprika, curry powder, coriander, pepper and garlic powder, then set aside half of the spice mixture for later. Use the remaining half to rub all over the inside and outside of the fish, then set aside. Set aside 2 tablespoons (8 g) of the parsley for garnish.

Heat a few tablespoons (30 ml) of oil in a pan over low heat, then add the onion. Cook the onion until slightly colored. Add the walnuts and stir until they turn golden. Add the remaining parsley and the cilantro and stir for a minute, then add the reserved spice mixture and the garlic and stir for another minute. Add the pomegranate molasses, mix well, then remove the pan from the heat.

Fill the inside of the fish with half of the onion mixture, then close the opening using threads or toothpicks. Rub the skin with some oil and sprinkle with salt. Cook the fish on the grill or middle rack of the oven until the fish skin is golden and the flesh is cooked.

Mix the reserved parsley with the juice from the remaining lime and a pinch of salt.

Serve the fish with the remaining half of the filling on the side. Drizzle the parsley sauce on top and sprinkle with pomegranate arils if desired.

# Rice & More

*There are many Persian culinary terms related to rice preparation, and some have been adopted by neighboring languages. The dish commonly referred to as pilaf in North America, pilau in Great Britain or pilav in Turkish has a Persian etymon:* pulaw.

*In modern Persian,* polo *is rice cooked in broth while the grains remain separate. To prepare polo, the half-cooked rice is drained before adding the broth, vegetables and meat, then "brewed" to perfection. Iranian cuisine boasts a range of rice dishes infused with various herbs and vegetables.*

Chelo *is white rice with separated grains and kateh is sticky rice.*

*During special occasions, saffron can be added to the rice to provide a beautiful yellow hue and a delightful saffron fragrance.*

*In this chapter, I have compiled several polo recipes from different regions of the country. Most vegetarian polo dishes can be combined with a meat dish. Each recipe includes common pairings, but if you are searching for a vegetarian option, they can stand alone as a complete and nutritious meal.*

# PERSIAN PLAIN RICE
## (Chelo/چلو)

*Chelo is a staple in Persian kitchens. Most of the dishes are accompanied by this fluffy, buttery long-grain rice. Persians can be meticulous regarding the quality and method of cooking rice. But once you learn the Persian way of cooking rice, you won't have it any other way.*

### SERVES 4

2 cups (400 g) basmati rice (see Note)

4 tbsp (72 g) salt, divided

2 tbsp (30 ml) cooking oil

2–4 tbsp (28–56 g) butter or ghee

**NOTE**

See the Rice section in the "Special Ingredients" chapter (page 13) to read more about rice and what kind to choose for the best results.

Put the rice in a big bowl and wash it under cold water. Rinse the rice seven to eight times, until the water is clear, then fill the bowl with more cold water until it covers the rice by about 1 inch (2.5 cm) on the top. Add 2 tablespoons (36 g) of salt and let the rice soak for at least 30 minutes or up to 4 hours before cooking.

Drain the rice. Bring 8½ cups (2 L) of water to a boil in a nonstick pot and add the remaining salt. Add the rice and let the water come to a boil again. Cook the rice for 5 to 10 minutes. Once you begin to see rice float to the top, try a grain. We are looking for an al dente texture—soft on the outside but a bit harder in the center. At this point, the rice grains will have grown longer in length compared to when they were raw. Empty the rice in a colander and briefly rinse it with cold water to remove the excess salt and stop any further cooking.

Rinse your pot and put it back on the stove. Add ⅓ cup (80 ml) of water and the oil and wait until the water boils. Scoop the rice back into the pot, making a dome shape. Keep the grains fluffy and avoid squishing them down. Make a few holes in the dome with the end of your spoon. These holes will allow the steam to pass from the bottom to the top. Put the lid back on the pot. Over medium-high heat, let the rice cook for about 5 minutes.

Once you see the steam rising from the rice, lower the heat, wrap the bottom of the lid in a kitchen towel or paper towel and put it back on the pot. The towel seals the pot, helps the steam cook the rice and absorbs the condensation, which stops the rice from getting soggy.

After 10 to 15 minutes, the rice is ready. You can check the doneness by quickly opening the lid and checking a grain. If you want to make *tahdig* (pages 42–46), let the rice cook on low for about 45 minutes.

Before serving, melt the butter and then add 2 tablespoons (30 ml) of hot water. Drizzle over the rice. Serve the chelo with kabaab or stews.

# PERSIAN CRISPY RICE THREE WAYS
## (ته دیگ/Tahdig)

*Tahdig translates to "the bottom of the pot," which refers to the crispy rice made on the bottom of the cooking pan while making steamed white rice or pilaf. Making tahdig is a way of avoiding waste and adding extra delicacy to a humble rice dish. There are many versions of tahdig that use different ingredients such as eggplant, onion, lettuce and potatoes. Here I explain the three most common ways of making tahdig.*

*The first recipe is made with simple white rice, but the following two are variations that you can use for any rice recipe provided in this book.*

## CHELO WITH YOGURT & SAFFRON CRISPY RICE
### (تهدیگ ماست/Tahdig Maast)

**SERVES 4**

Persian Plain Rice (page 41)

¼ cup (75 g) Greek yogurt

⅛ tsp powdered saffron

Pinch of salt

2–3 tbsp (30–45 ml) cooking oil

2–4 tbsp (28–56 g) butter, cubed

Follow the directions for making chelo up to boiling and rinsing the rice. Rinse your pot and put it back on the stove. Mix the yogurt with the saffron and a pinch of salt in a medium bowl. Once well mixed, take 1 cup (160 g) of the drained cooked rice and gently fold in the yogurt mix.

Add the oil to the hot pot. Layer the rice and yogurt mixture at the bottom. Press down gently with the bottom of a spoon to make it firm. Scoop the rest of the rice on top of this layer, creating a dome shape. Keep the grains fluffy and avoid squishing them down. Make a few holes in the dome with the end of your spoon and put the lid back on. Over medium-high heat, let the rice cook for about 5 minutes.

Once you see the steam rising from the rice, put the heat on low, lay the butter cubes on top, wrap the bottom of the lid in a kitchen towel or paper towel and put it back on the pot. The towel seals the pot, helps the steam cook the rice and absorbs the condensation, which stops the tahdig from getting soggy.

Let the rice cook on low for 35 to 45 minutes. Take the lid off and cover the pot with a large round serving tray slightly wider than the pot. Flip the rice onto the tray. The crispy yogurt saffron tahdig will be at the top. Serve with stews or kabaab.

# BREAD & SAFFRON CRISPY BOTTOM
## (Tahdig Naan/نان تهدیگ)

*Tahdig Naan is usually made with a thin layer of naan lavash spread under the rice at the bottom of the pot. This thin, crispy fried layer is what people will fight for at the dinner table. However, given that lavash bread is not widely available in Western countries, using a mix of flour and water is an excellent substitute. If you have lavash, simply cut it into small pieces and cover the bottom of the pot with them instead of the mixture below.*

## SERVES 4–6

FOR AN 8-INCH
(20-CM)-WIDE POT

Persian Plain Rice (page 41)

Pinch of powdered saffron
(optional)

2 tbsp (16 g) flour

A pinch of salt

Cooking oil, as needed

FOR A 10-INCH
(25-CM)-WIDE POT

Persian Plain Rice (page 41)

Pinch of powdered saffron
(optional)

⅔ cup (160 ml) cold water

4 tbsp (32 g) flour

Pinch of salt

Cooking oil, as needed

Follow the directions for making chelo up to boiling and rinsing the rice. You can also make the rice using any of the other recipes in this chapter.

If using, let the saffron brew in ⅓ cup (80 ml) cold water for about 10 minutes. Next, add the flour and a pinch of salt and mix well until combined. After boiling the rice and before piling it in the pot for the final steaming, add a few tablespoons (30 ml) of oil to the pot and pour the flour mixture on top, then evenly spread it.

Once the mixture begins to solidify (like a crepe), pile the rice over it. Do not press down, as you want to keep the grains fluffy. Next, make a few holes in the rice with the bottom of a spoon. Cover the bottom of the lid with a kitchen towel or paper towel and put it back on the pot, then reduce the heat to medium-low and cook for 30 to 40 minutes.

If using a nonstick pot, the rice can be flipped over into a serving dish with the golden, crispy tahdig on top. Otherwise, serve the rice in a serving tray, then separate the tahdig from the bottom of the pan and serve it separately.

# CRISPY POTATO BOTTOM OF THE POT

(تهدیگ سیب زمینی/Tahdig Sibzamini)

*Using vegetables is also a common way of making tahdig. Potatoes are one of the most common vegetables to use. Their subtle starchy flavor makes them perfect with any dish without adding a contradictory taste. They turn crispy and golden, slowly frying under the rice, and are an irresistible addition to any stew dish.*

## SERVES 4

Pinch of saffron (optional)

Persian Plain Rice (page 41)

Cooking oil, as needed

11 oz (300 g) potatoes, peeled and cut into ½" (1.3-cm) thick disks

Pinch of salt

If using the saffron, add it to a small bowl with 2 to 3 tablespoons (30 to 45 ml) cold water and let it sit for 5 minutes.

Follow the directions for making the rice up to boiling and rinsing. Then add a few tablespoons (30 ml) of oil to the pot, and arrange the potato disks at the bottom to cover it completely. Do not overlay the potatoes.

Drizzle the brewed saffron over the potatoes, sprinkle with some salt, then layer the rice over top. Put the lid back and cook over medium heat until steam rises when you open the lid. Wrap the bottom of the lid with a kitchen towel or paper towel and put it back on. Continue cooking over medium-low heat for 30 to 40 minutes.

If your pot is nonstick, you should be able to flip the rice over like a cake onto a big plate. Otherwise, serve the rice in a serving tray, then separate the potatoes using a spatula and serve on the side.

# RAINBOW RICE WITH LAMB

## (Qeymeh Nesaar/قیمه نثار)

*This dish comes from Qazvin, one of the most historical cities in Iran. Qeymeh Nesaar is a buttery long-grain rice dish garnished with nuts, sour berries and saffron, which is then served with a tender lamb goulash cooked with subtle aromatic spices. I love this dish so much for how balanced yet impactful all the flavors are.*

### SERVES 4

⅛ tsp powdered saffron

Cooking oil, as needed

2 onions, finely chopped

1.1 lb (500 g) lamb stew meat, cut into small chunks

6–8 cardamom pods

2 tsp (5 g) ground turmeric

2 tsp (5 g) ground cinnamon

½ tsp ground black pepper

2 tbsp (32 g) tomato paste

3¼ cups (750 ml) water, plus more as needed

Salt, as needed

2 cups (400 g) Persian Plain Rice (page 41)

Peel of 2 oranges (see Notes)

2.8 oz (80 g) barberries (see Notes)

2 oz (60 g) slivered almonds or a mix of slivered almonds and slivered pistachios

3 tbsp (39 g) + 2 tsp (9 g) sugar, divided

1 tsp rose water (optional, see Notes)

2–3 tbsp (30–45 ml) vegetable oil

Add 4 tablespoons (60 ml) cold water to the saffron in a small bowl and set aside to brew.

In a medium pot over medium heat, heat a few tablespoons (30 ml) of oil, then cook the onions until lightly golden. Add the lamb and sear until slightly browned. Crack the cardamom pods open just a little, then add them along with the turmeric, cinnamon and black pepper to the pot. Cook for a minute until fragrant.

Add the tomato paste and stir for another minute until the paste turns darker in color. Add the water, then bring to a boil. Cover the pot with a lid and cook over medium-low heat until the lamb is fully cooked and tender, 1 to 2 hours. Check the stew every 30 minutes and add more water if needed. After the first 30 minutes, taste, and add salt if needed.

Meanwhile, prepare the rice using the chelo recipe (page 41).

While the rice and meat are cooking, cut off the white part of the orange peels, then cut them into matchsticks. In a small pot, bring 2 cups (480 ml) of water to a boil. Cook the orange peels for 10 to 15 minutes. Drain, rinse and set aside in a cold cup of water. Wash the barberries and slivered nuts, then soak them in a cup (240 ml) of water and set aside.

The stew is ready when the meat is tender and the sauce thickens. If the meat is cooked but the sauce is thin, cook on high heat with no lid for a few minutes, while watching, to reduce the sauce. Once the stew is ready, stir in 2 teaspoons (9 g) of sugar and the rose water (if using). Cook for another minute until the sugar is dissolved.

When your rice is ready, put 2 cups (320 g) of the cooked rice in a bowl and add the brewed saffron. With a fork, gently fold the rice with the saffron to mix well. Avoid overmixing, as it can break the rice grains and make them mushy.

(continued)

# RAINBOW RICE WITH LAMB
*(continued)*

Drain the barberries, nuts and orange peels, then add them to a hot pan with the vegetable oil. Add 3 tablespoons (39 g) of sugar and mix to combine. Cook for 2 to 3 minutes, until slightly colored and the sugar has dissolved.

Serve the rice in a serving tray, then layer the saffron rice and the mix of nuts and berries on top. Spoon the meat and sauce over everything and serve.

---

**NOTES**

The rose water amount is so little that it is barely noticeable, but it adds a nice layer to the aromas; if you don't have it, you can omit it.

You can replace the orange peels with the zest of 2 oranges and add them to the pan when frying the berries and nuts.

The barberries can be replaced with dried cranberries chopped into small pieces. If your dried cranberries are already sweetened, skip the 3 tablespoons (39 g) of sugar added to the berries.

---

# MUNG BEAN, TAHINI & DATE RICE
## (Maash va Ardeh Polo/ماش و ارده پلو)

*A vegetarian dish from Khuzestan in the south of Iran, Maash va Ardeh Polo is an ultimate comfort food that comes together in no time. Mung beans are considered an ancient superfood because of their high nutritional value and health benefits, and this recipe makes you love them even more.*

### SERVES 4

½ cup (100 g) dried green mung beans

1½ cups (300 g) basmati rice

2 tbsp (36 g) salt, divided, plus more as needed

1 tsp Rice Mixed Spices (page 21)

Cooking oil, as needed

1¼ cups (200 g) onions, halved and thinly sliced

7 oz (200 g) pitted dates

¼ cup (60 g) dark tahini (see Notes)

Wash the mung beans and soak them in water for at least 30 minutes. Wash the rice seven to eight times with cold water in a bowl until the water runs clear. Fill the bowl with water and add 1 tablespoon (18 g) of salt. Let the rice soak in the bowl for at least 30 minutes.

Meanwhile, drain and rinse the mung beans. In a pot, cook the mung beans with enough water to cover them and a pinch of salt until soft. Make sure not to overcook the beans, as they will lose their shape. Drain the mung beans, rinse with cold water and set aside.

Bring 8½ cups (2 L) of water to a boil in a pot about 10 inches (25 cm) wide and add the remaining salt. Drain the rice and cook it in the boiling water for 8 to 10 minutes. Try a grain; it should be longer and cooked with a slightly hard center. Drain the rice and rinse briefly with cold water to wash off the excess salt. In a bowl, gently combine the rice with the mixed spices and cooked mung beans using a fork. Avoid mixing too much or crushing the rice.

If you would like to make tahdig (the crispy bottom), rinse the pot and put it back on the stove. Add a few tablespoons (30 ml) of cooking oil, and follow the recipe instructions on page 42.

If you don't want to make tahdig, gently pile the rice and beans in the hot pot in a dome shape. Keep it fluffy, and don't press the rice down. Make a few holes in the dome with the end of a spoon. Drizzle ¼ cup (60 ml) of water over the top, then cover the bottom of the lid with a kitchen towel or paper towel and put it tightly on the pot. Cook over medium heat for about 5 minutes, then reduce to low and cook for another 15 minutes.

(continued)

# MUNG BEAN, TAHINI & DATE RICE
*(continued)*

Heat a few tablespoons (30 ml) of oil in a pan over medium heat, then add the onions. Cook the onions until they are golden and caramelized, then add the dates and fry for another 2 minutes, stirring occasionally. Remove the onions and dates from the heat and set aside. Reserve the oil in the pan.

Mix the tahini with 7 tablespoons (100 ml) of cold water. Keep stirring and add cold water, 1 tablespoon (15 ml) at a time if needed, until it has a drizzling consistency.

Serve the rice garnished with the caramelized onions and dates. Spoon the reserved oil from the pan over the rice and drizzle on the tahini. This salty and sweet meal pairs well with spicy condiments like pickled peppers or vegetables.

---

**NOTES**

Dark tahini is made from roasted sesame seeds. Look for the words "roasted" or "toasted" on the label.

As tahini is oily, do not add oil to the rice while steaming.

---

# SPICY SHRIMP RICE WITH TAMARIND
## (Meygoo Polo/میگو پلو)

*Dishes from south Iran are warm and welcoming, like its people. Having the Persian Gulf on one side means abundant fresh seafood is available. Also, given the warm climate of the southern states, spices are used generously; the more, the better. The spicier the food, the more you sweat and the better your body can cool down. Spices combined with seafood create dishes that are difficult to resist and harder to forget. There are a few variations of meygoo polo throughout the southern states. This version is my favorite.*

### SERVES 4

1½ cups (300 g) basmati rice

3 tbsp (54 g) salt, divided, plus more as needed

½ cup (45 g) chopped cilantro, divided, plus more for garnish

1 tbsp (11 g) dried fenugreek, divided

Cooking oil, as needed

1¼ cups (200 g) onions, halved and thinly sliced

5 cloves garlic, chopped

14 oz (400 g) shrimp, shelled and cleaned

Ground black pepper, as needed

2 tbsp (13 g) hot or mild curry powder

1 tbsp (7 g) paprika

2 tbsp (15 g) tamarind paste without seeds

1 tbsp (13 g) sugar (optional)

⅛ tsp powdered saffron

2 tbsp (28 g) butter or ghee

Wash the rice seven to eight times with cold water in a bowl until the water runs clear. Fill the bowl with cold water until it covers the rice by about 1 inch (2.5 cm). Add 1 tablespoon (18 g) of salt and let the rice soak for at least 30 minutes and up to 4 hours.

Meanwhile, bring 8½ cups (2 L) of water to a boil in a nonstick pot and add the remaining salt. Once boiling, drain the soaked rice and add it to the pot. Bring the water to a boil again, then reduce the heat to medium.

Depending on the rice brand, the rice can take 5 to 10 minutes to cook. Once you see the rice start to float to the top, try a grain. We are looking for an al dente texture—soft on the outside but a bit harder in the center. At this point, the rice grains should also be longer. Empty the rice in a colander and briefly rinse with cold water to remove any excess salt and stop the cooking process.

Set aside a quarter of the cilantro for garnish. Mix the remaining three-quarters of the cilantro with half of the dried fenugreek, then gently stir the mixture into the rice.

Rinse the pot and put it back on the stove. Add ⅓ cup (80 ml) of water and 2 tablespoons (30 ml) of oil and bring the water to a boil over high heat. Scoop the rice back into the pot, making a dome shape. Keep the grains fluffy and avoid squishing them down. Make a few holes in the dome with the end of your spoon. These holes allow the steam to pass from the bottom of the pot to the top. Cover the pot with a lid.

(continued)

# SPICY SHRIMP RICE WITH TAMARIND

*(continued)*

Over medium-high heat, let the rice cook for about 5 minutes. Once you see the steam rising from the rice, put it over low heat, wrap the bottom of the lid in a kitchen towel or paper towel and put it back on the pot. Let the rice cook on low for about 45 minutes if you want to make tahdig (page 42). Otherwise, the rice will be ready in about 15 minutes.

While the rice is cooking, in a nonstick pan over medium heat, cook the onions with 1 to 2 tablespoons (15 to 30 ml) of oil until golden and caramelized. Add the garlic, then cook for another minute. Take them out of the pan and set aside.

In the same pan, fry the shrimp, seasoned with salt and pepper, over high heat. Stir frequently and add the curry powder, paprika and the remaining half of the dried fenugreek. Stir until the spices are fragrant. Add the onions and garlic back to the pan. Add the tamarind paste and ½ cup (118 ml) of water, and mix everything well. Taste the sauce, and if it's too sour, add sugar. Bring the sauce to a boil, then turn it off and set aside.

Mix the saffron with 3 tablespoons (45 ml) cold water in a small bowl and let it sit for 5 minutes. Melt the butter and add to the bowl with the saffron. Once the rice is cooked, drizzle the butter and saffron mixture over the rice and gently fold in. Serve the rice with the shrimp sauce and garnish with extra cilantro.

# GREEN BEANS & BEEF PILAF
### (Loobiyaa Polo/لوبیا پلو)

*Loobiyaa polo is one of the most loved Persian dishes across the country. Basmati rice layered with a thick tomato-based sauce along with beef, green beans and aromatic spices come together to create a comforting meal.*

## SERVES 4

2 cups (400 g) basmati rice

3 tbsp (54 g) salt, divided, plus more as needed

⅛ tsp powdered saffron

Cooking oil, as needed

1½ cups (150 g) green beans, trimmed and cut into 1" (2.5-cm) pieces

1 cup (150 g) yellow onion, finely chopped

2 tsp (6 g) ground turmeric

¼ tsp ground black pepper

½ tsp paprika

2 tsp (5 g) ground cinnamon

1 tsp Rice Mixed Spices (page 21, optional)

11 oz (300 g) ground beef

5 tbsp (75 g) tomato paste

10.6 oz (300 g) potatoes (optional, see Notes)

2 tbsp (28 g) butter (optional, see Notes)

Wash the rice in a bowl under cold water seven to eight times, until the water runs clear. Fill the bowl with water, add 1 tablespoon (18 g) of salt and let the rice soak for at least 30 minutes.

Add the saffron to a bowl with ⅓ cup (80 ml) cold water and let it brew.

Heat a few tablespoons (30 ml) of oil in a large pan and cook the green beans briefly until they get slightly colored. Take them out of the pan and set aside.

Cook the onion in the same pan until golden. Add the turmeric, pepper, paprika, cinnamon and rice spices (if using) to the pan and stir for a minute. Add the ground beef, breaking it apart with your spoon, and mix everything well. Cook the meat until it has browned, then add the tomato paste and mix well again. Cook the mixture for 2 to 3 minutes, until the paste becomes darker in color. Add the green beans back to the pan along with some salt and the water, and stir until a sauce forms. Reduce the heat to low and let it cook for another 5 to 10 minutes, then turn off and set aside.

Meanwhile, bring 8½ cups (2 L) of water to a boil in a 10-inch (25-cm) pot and add 2 tablespoons (36 g) of salt. If you are using potatoes, while the water is boiling, peel the potatoes and cut them into ½-inch (1.3-cm)-thick disks, then set aside. Drain the rice and add it to the boiling water. Cook for 8 to 10 minutes, until the grains are visibly longer and soft with a slightly harder center. Drain the rice and briefly rinse with cold water. Rinse out the pot and return it to the stove.

Add a few tablespoons (30 ml) of oil to the pot, then arrange the potato disks to cover the bottom completely. Do not overlay the potatoes. Cover the potatoes with a layer of rice, drizzle with some of the brewed saffron and add a layer of the meat-and-beans sauce. Briefly mix the rice and the sauce with a fork (you don't need to mix them well).

(continued)

# GREEN BEANS & BEEF PILAF
*(continued)*

Continue layering the rice, saffron and sauce. In the top layer of rice, create a few holes in the rice using the end of a spoon. Put the lid on and cook on medium heat until steam rises when you open the lid. Once you see the steam, cut the butter (if using) into small pieces and spread it over the rice. Wrap the bottom of the lid with a kitchen towel or paper towel and put it back on tightly. Continue cooking over medium-low heat for 30 to 40 minutes.

If your pot is nonstick, you should be able to flip over the rice like a cake onto a big plate. Otherwise, serve the rice in a serving tray, then separate the potatoes using a spatula and serve them on the side. This pilaf pairs well with Yogurt and Cucumber Dip (page 143) or Shirazi Salad (page 151).

---

**NOTES**

Using potatoes for the bottom to make tahdig is optional, but I highly recommend it as not only does the aromatic oil released from the sauce make them extra delicious, but also, because of the tomato-based sauce, the rice can get burned at the bottom quickly if there isn't a layer of potatoes. Alternatively, you can make the version of tahdig from Bread and Saffron Crispy Bottom (page 45).

As the sauce has some oil, adding butter or oil to the rice at the time of steaming is optional, but adding a little bit of butter makes the dish a lot more appetizing.

---

# LENTIL RICE WITH RAISINS & GROUND BEEF
## (عدس پلو/Adas Polo)

*Lentil rice, garnished with caramelized onion and raisins and mixed with aromatic spices, is a whole vegetarian meal on its own. There are different variations of it also being served with ground beef, chicken or fried dates on the side. I am sharing the beef version here, but feel free to skip the meat and make it vegetarian.*

### SERVES 4

½ cup (150 g) brown lentils

1½ cups (300 g) basmati rice

3 tbsp (54 g) salt, divided, plus more as needed

⅛ tsp powdered saffron (optional)

⅔ cup (100 g) black or red raisins

1 tbsp (8 g) Rice Mixed Spices (page 21, see Notes)

Cooking oil, as needed

2 tbsp (28 g) butter (optional)

½ cup (80 g) finely chopped yellow onion (see Notes)

1½ tsp (5 g) ground turmeric

1 tsp Stew Mixed Spices (page 22, optional)

½ lb (250 g) ground beef

Black pepper, to taste

⅔ cup (30 g) Persian-Style Crispy Fried Onions (page 25) or store-bought crispy onions

Wash the lentils and soak them in a bowl with enough water to cover them fully for about 30 minutes—soaking them reduces cooking time and makes them easier to digest. Wash the rice in a bowl with cold water seven to eight times, until the water is clear. Fill the bowl with cold water until it covers the rice by about 1 inch (2.5 cm). Add 1 tablespoon (18 g) of salt and soak the rice for about 30 minutes. If using the saffron, add it to a small bowl with 4 tablespoons (60 ml) of cold water and set aside. Wash the raisins and soak them in water in a small bowl.

Over medium to high heat, cook the lentils in a pot with about 3 cups (750 ml) of water and ½ teaspoon of salt. Cook until the lentils are soft but still have their shape, 10 to 15 minutes. They will cook further with the rice, and overcooking can spoil the look of the finished dish. Drain the lentils and rinse them briefly with cold water to stop the cooking process, then set aside.

In a 10-inch (25-cm)-wide pot, bring 8½ cups (2 L) of water to a boil. Drain the soaked rice and add it to the boiling water with 2 tablespoons (36 g) of salt. Cook for 8 to 10 minutes, until the rice grains are visibly longer and soft with a slightly harder center. Drain the rice and briefly rinse with cold water. Add the lentils and Rice Mixed Spices to the rice and mix gently with a fork.

Put the pot back on the stove. Add a few tablespoons (30 ml) of oil, then pile the rice into the pot in a dome shape. Keep the grains fluffy and avoid pressing down. Create a few holes in the rice with the bottom of a spoon to let the steam freely pass from the bottom of the pot to the top. Put the lid on and cook for about 10 minutes over medium heat. Then cut the butter (if using) into small cubes (or use a few spoons of cooking oil) and scatter over the rice. Cover the lid with a kitchen or paper towel and put it back on the pot. Then reduce the heat to low and cook for another 15 to 20 minutes.

(continued)

Heat a few tablespoons (30 ml) of oil in a pan over medium heat. Drain the raisins and add them to the pan. Cook for 1 to 2 minutes, until they are puffy. Take them out of the pan and set aside.

Cook the onion in a pan with a few tablespoons (30 ml) of oil until slightly colored. Add the turmeric and Stew Mixed Spices (if using) and stir for a minute. Add the ground beef and brown until thoroughly cooked. Sprinkle the beef mixture with salt and pepper, then take it off the heat.

Before serving, mix the meat and saffron into the lentil rice, gently folding it in with a spoon. Garnish the rice with crispy onions and raisins. This dish pairs well with Shirazi Salad (page 151) and Yogurt and Cucumber Dip (page 143).

---

NOTES

You can replace the 1 tablespoon (8 g) of the Rice Mixed Spices with ½ tablespoon (4 g) of ground cinnamon.

The onion mentioned in the ingredients is to flavor the beef. If you are not including beef in this dish, you can remove the onion.

---

# CARROT RICE WITH CHICKEN THIGHS

## (Havij Polo/هویج پلو)

*This pilaf consists of caramelized carrots layered in basmati rice and served with chicken thighs cooked in aromatic spices. It is an irresistible combination of sweet, salty and gentle spices.*

### SERVES 4

2½ cups (500 g) basmati rice

3 tbsp + 1 tsp (59 g) salt, divided

Cooking oil, as needed

4 skinless chicken thighs

1 tbsp (9 g) ground turmeric

1 tsp mild curry powder

½ tsp whole black peppercorn

4 bay leaves

1 small carrot, cut into 1" (2.5-cm) chunks

1 celery stick, cut into 1" (2.5-cm) chunks

4½ cups (500 g) shredded carrots

2 tbsp (26 g) + 2 tsp (9 g) sugar

⅔ lb (300 g) potatoes, peeled and thinly sliced (optional)

2 tsp (5 g) Rice Mixed Spices (page 21)

1 oz (30 g) barberries (optional)

3 tbsp (20 g) slivered pistachios (optional)

Wash the rice in a bowl with cold water seven to eight times, until the water is clear. Fill the bowl with cold water until it covers the rice. Add 1 tablespoon (18 g) of salt and let the rice soak for at least 30 minutes.

Heat a few tablespoons (30 ml) of oil in a large pan with a lid over medium-high heat. Cook both sides of the chicken thighs until golden. Add the turmeric, curry powder, black peppercorn and bay leaves to the oil and turn the chicken thighs to coat them in the spices. Add the carrot and celery chunks to the pot. Add 1 cup (240 ml) of water and 1 teaspoon of salt to the pot, then cover with the lid and let cook over medium-low heat for about 45 minutes.

Meanwhile, in a different pan, heat a few tablespoons (30 ml) of oil over medium heat. Add the shredded carrots to the pan and cook for about 5 minutes, stirring occasionally. Once the carrots are wilted, sprinkle in the sugar and pour in ¼ cup (60 ml) water. Cover the pan with a lid and cook over medium-low heat for 10 to 15 minutes, stirring occasionally, to caramelize the carrots.

Bring 8½ cups (2 L) of water to a boil in a nonstick pot and add 2 tablespoons (36 g) of salt. Drain the rice and add it to the boiling water. Cook for 8 to 10 minutes, until the grains are longer and soft and have a slightly hard center (try a grain to be sure). Drain the rice and briefly rinse with cold water.

(continued)

# CARROT RICE WITH CHICKEN THIGHS
*(continued)*

Put the same pot back on the stove. Add a few tablespoons (30 ml) of oil to the pot, then arrange the potatoes on the bottom without overlapping. Layer the rice and shredded carrots over the potatoes, sprinkling each layer with the Rice Mixed Spices, and very gently mix with a fork (it does not need to be well mixed). Keep the rice fluffy and avoid squishing it down. Put the lid back and cook over medium heat for about 10 minutes, until you see steam rising from the rice when opening the top. Then cover the bottom of the lid with a kitchen towel or paper towel and put it back on the pot. Cook for another 30 minutes over medium-low heat.

If using barberries, before serving, wash and cook them for 2 to 3 minutes with 2 teaspoons (9 g) of sugar in a pan over medium heat.

Sprinkle the rice with the barberries and pistachios, if desired, before serving. Discard the carrot and celery sticks from the chicken broth, then serve the chicken with the reduced broth on the side.

# SAFFRON, YOGURT & CHICKEN RICE PILAF
## (Tahchin Morgh/تهچین مرغ)

*One of the most well-known Persian dishes among Westerners is* tahchin. *It is a saffron rice cake with a crispy top, layered with tender marinated chicken pieces and finished with sautéed barberries—a dish with subtle yet profound flavors that is hard to pass up.*

### SERVES 4

2 cups (400 g) basmati rice

3 tbsp (54 g) salt, divided, plus more as needed

¼ tsp saffron powder

2½ oz (70 g) dried barberries (see Notes)

Cooking oil, as needed

1 cup (150 g) finely chopped yellow onion

4 skinless and boneless chicken thighs

1 tsp ground turmeric

Black pepper, as needed

2 bay leaves

2 egg yolks

½ cup (150 g) Greek yogurt

2 tbsp (25 g) butter (optional)

2 tbsp (26 g) sugar

2 tbsp (13 g) slivered pistachios, for garnish (optional)

Wash the rice in a big bowl seven to eight times, until the water rinses clear. Then fill the bowl with water and 1 tablespoon (18 g) salt and let the rice soak for at least 30 minutes.

Next, add the saffron and 2 to 3 tablespoons (30 to 45 ml) cold water in a ramekin and let it brew. Wash the barberries, soak them in water and set aside.

Add a few tablespoons (30 ml) of oil to a nonstick pan and cook the onion until lightly colored. Remove the onion from the pan and set aside. In the same pan, cook the chicken thighs over medium-high heat until both sides are perfectly seared and golden, adding more oil to the pan if needed. Add the onion back to the pan along with the turmeric, a pinch of salt and pepper. Stir for a minute, then add the bay leaves and 1 cup (240 ml) of water. Cover with a lid and cook on medium-low until the chicken thighs are tender and the broth has reduced and thickened. Set the chicken thighs aside and discard the broth.

In a large nonstick pot, bring 8½ cups (2 L) of water to a boil and add 2 tablespoons (36 g) of salt. Drain the soaked rice and add it to the boiling water. Cook for 8 to 10 minutes on high heat until the rice grains float to the top. The grains will be visibly longer and if you taste a grain, it should be soft with a slightly hard center. Drain the rice and briefly rinse with cold water.

In a large bowl, mix the egg yolks with the yogurt, brewed saffron and a pinch of salt and pepper. Stir until combined, then gently fold in the cooked rice.

(continued)

# SAFFRON, YOGURT & CHICKEN RICE PILAF
## *(continued)*

Heat the previously used rice pot over high heat. Add a few tablespoons (30 ml) of oil to the pot and reduce the heat to medium. Add half of the rice mixture to the bottom of the pot. With the back of a spoon, gently press down to flatten the rice. Layer the cooked chicken over the rice. Add the remaining rice on top and gently press down with the back of your spoon. Make a few holes in the rice with the end of the spoon, but don't go all the way down to the pot. Cover with a lid and cook on medium heat for about 10 minutes. Then reduce the heat to medium-low and cook for 30 to 45 minutes.

Meanwhile, rinse the soaked barberries. In a small pan on medium heat, add 1 tablespoon (15 ml) of oil and the butter (if using). Add the barberries and sprinkle with the sugar. Sauté, stirring until the sugar dissolves and the berries puff up. Remove the pan from heat to avoid burning the sugar and making it bitter.

Cover the pot of rice with a large round serving tray that is wider than your pot and flip the rice into the tray. Garnish with the barberries and pistachios (if using) and serve.

---

### NOTES

If you don't have barberries, use dried cranberries. Chop them small and sauté with butter.

If the cranberries are sweetened, skip adding the sugar.

---

# BROAD BEAN & DILL PILAF
## (باقالی پلو/Baaqaali Polo)

*Baaqaali polo is one of the most famous rice dishes in Iran. It is a complete vegan meal on its own but also pairs perfectly with all kinds of meat. The most common pairing with it is braised lamb shank, which you can find the recipe for on page 84.*

*Other delicious pairings include Chicken Kabaab (page 32) or fried salmon.*

### SERVES 4

1½ cups (300 g) basmati rice

3 tbsp (54 g) salt, divided

1 cup (220 g) fresh or frozen broad beans, shelled and peeled

¼ tsp ground turmeric

½ cup (40 g) fresh dill, finely chopped

¼ tsp ground cinnamon

Cooking oil, as needed

2 tbsp (28 g) butter or vegetable oil for a dairy-free option

Wash the rice with cold water in a bowl seven to eight times, until the water runs clear. Soak the rice with 1 tablespoon (18 g) of salt in a bowl with cold water, enough to stand about 1 inch (2.5 cm) above the rice. Let the rice soak for at least 30 minutes and up to 4 hours.

Bring 8½ cups (2 L) of water to a boil in a medium pot and add the remaining salt. Drain the soaked rice, add it to the boiling water and bring it back to a boil. Watch the rice until the grains start floating to the top, 5 to 10 minutes. Test a grain, and once it is soft with a slightly hard center, add the broad beans and turmeric. Boil for a minute, then drain the rice and rinse briefly with cold water to remove any excess salt.

In a large bowl, add the rice with the dill and cinnamon and mix gently with a fork. Rinse the pot that was previously used, and put it back on the stove over medium heat. Heat a few tablespoons (30 ml) of oil in the pot. Pile the rice into a dome shape in the pot without pushing it down. The rice grains should be light and fluffy and not pressed. Create a few holes with the end of your spoon in the dome. Cover with a lid and cook over medium heat for about 5 minutes, until you see steam rising. Cut the butter into small cubes and distribute them over the rice. Cover the bottom of the lid with a kitchen towel or paper towel and put it back on the pot. Cook the rice for 20 to 30 minutes over low heat.

Serve the rice on its own or with a side of salad or pickles, or enjoy with your choice of meat.

### NOTE
This recipe makes the rice without tahdig (the crispy bottom). If you'd like to make tahdig, follow the recipe on page 42.

# Stews of All Kinds

*Cooking stew goes back to ancient times, and in Persian cuisine, stews have become a primary cooking method.*

*Persian stews usually include meat (lamb or beef), herbs and various types of beans. However, fish, duck, chicken, nuts, fruits and vegetables are also frequently used in different regions. To bring out all the flavors and achieve a tender meat texture, the traditional method is to slow cook the stews. However, many new generations are more health-conscious and try to retain the nutrients of herbs and vegetables by adopting shorter cooking times.*

*This chapter features recipes from various corners of the country, each with unique flavors and ingredient profiles. While stews are typically paired with rice, bread can also serve as a tasty substitute if desired.*

# HERBY BEAN STEW WITH SMOKED FISH
### (Baaqla Qaatoq/باقلا قاتوق)

*Baaqlaa qaatoq is a famous, simple yet flavorful vegetarian stew from northern Iran made of split beans that are local to the Caspian Sea–neighboring provinces but can be easily made with any other beans in a similar family, like fresh borlotti or pinto beans. Traditionally, this dish is served with smoked or salted dry fish on the side, which adds a layer of umami to the flavors. For a vegetarian option, you can skip the fish or serve it with some fermented veggies—I love it with kimchi.*

## SERVES 4

1¾ cups (350 g) basmati rice

1 tbsp (18 g) + ½ tsp salt, divided, plus more as needed

1 cup (400 g) fresh borlotti beans (see Note)

1 (9-oz [250-g]) smoked trout or mackerel

¼ cup (60 g) butter

Cooking oil, as needed

8 cloves garlic, finely chopped

2 tsp (6 g) ground turmeric

1¼ cups (100 g) fresh dill or 5 tbsp (15 g) dried

Black pepper, to taste

4 eggs

Sliced turnips, pickled veggies or black garlic, to serve

### NOTE

Alternatively, you can use dry beans for this stew. If so, cut the amount in half to 1 cup (200 g). You will need to soak the dry beans overnight or at least 12 hours before cooking until you can peel them. The cooking time may increase when using dried beans.

Wash the rice in a large bowl with cold water seven to eight times, until the water runs clear. Add water to the bowl until it covers the rice by about 1 inch (2.5 cm). Add 1 tablespoon (18 g) of salt to the rice and let it soak for at least 30 minutes.

Meanwhile, shell the beans out of their second skin. To make this process easier, you can soak the beans in water for an hour beforehand. Rinse the soaked rice and add it to a pot with enough water to cover the rice by about 1 inch (2.5 cm). Add ½ teaspoon of salt.

Cook the rice over medium-high heat until all the water is evaporated. If using smoked fish, cut it into four pieces, put them on a small plate and place the fish with the plate on top of the rice. The fish will warm up with steam while the rice cooks. Cover the bottom of the lid with a kitchen towel or paper towel and put it back on the pot. Cook the rice on low for about 15 minutes, until the grains are soft.

Meanwhile, in another pot, melt the butter over medium heat and add a tablespoon (15 ml) of oil to stop the butter from browning. Add the garlic and stir for a minute until fragrant. Stir in the beans and turmeric and cook for a couple more minutes, then add the dill and cook for a minute more. Add 9½ cups (2¼ L) of water and cover the pot with a lid. Cook for 10 to 15 minutes. Try a bean, and if it's soft, add salt and pepper. This stew is meant to have little water. If there is too much liquid, let it boil without a lid for a few minutes, until the sauce thickens.

Make a few holes in the stew with a spoon and break the eggs into the holes. Cover with the lid again and cook on low until the eggs are cooked. Serve the stew with the rice and flake the smoked fish on top. Add fresh turnips, pickled veggies or black garlic on the side for extra deliciousness.

# WALNUT, PUMPKIN & POMEGRANATE STEW

(Kadoo Fesenjan/کدو فسنجان)

*This vegetarian dish from northern Iran is nutritious and has unique flavors that are hard to match. This dish looks very similar to fesenjan, another beloved stew known in the West, but the spices are different and it doesn't have chicken. This dish in the Gilaki language (the language spoken in northern provinces in Iran) is called* kouyi tare *and is served with white rice or naan.*

## SERVES 4

1¾ cups (220 g) walnuts

Cooking oil, as needed

1 cup (200 g) finely chopped yellow onion

3–6 tbsp (63–126 g) pomegranate molasses (see Note)

1⅔ lb (750 g) pumpkin or butternut squash

Salt and pepper, to taste

1 tbsp (13 g) sugar

1 tbsp (9 g) Persian hogweed powder

1 tsp ground turmeric

1 tbsp (2 g) dried mint

4 tbsp (20 g) crushed walnuts, to garnish (optional)

4 tbsp (44 g) pomegranate arils, to garnish (optional)

Cooked rice or bread, to serve

Grind the walnuts in a food processor until it reaches a coarse flour consistency. In a pan over medium heat, toast the walnut flour until slightly colored and fragrant, then set aside.

Heat a few tablespoons (30 ml) of oil in a pot. Add the onion to the pot and cook over low heat until golden. Then add the toasted walnut flour to the pot and mix. Start by adding 3 tablespoons (63 g) of the pomegranate molasses to the pot. Add 2¾ cups (650 ml) cold water and bring to a boil. Put the lid on and cook over low heat for about 1 hour, stirring the sauce every 20 minutes.

Preheat the oven to 374°F (190°C). Cut the pumpkin open and take the seeds out. Discard the seeds. Roast the pumpkin in the oven for 15 to 20 minutes, until cooked. Alternatively, you can steam it. Scoop the meat out of the pumpkin and discard the skin. Puree the pumpkin meat in a food processor, then set aside.

After about 1 hour, the walnuts will release their oil, making the sauce darker and thicker. Taste the sauce and add more pomegranate molasses if needed, 1 tablespoon (21 g) at a time. Add the salt, pepper, sugar, Persian hogweed and pumpkin puree to the sauce and mix well.

In a small pan, heat 1 tablespoon (15 ml) of oil. Add the turmeric and mint, then turn the heat off. Let the spices sizzle for about a minute while stirring. Stir the turmeric and mint into the stew. Cook the stew over low heat with the lid on for another 15 minutes.

Garnish the stew with the crushed walnuts and pomegranate arils, if desired, and serve with rice or bread.

> ### NOTE
> Depending on the quality and density of the pomegranate molasses, you may need more or less of it. Start with 3 tablespoons (63 g) and add more to your liking.

# CELERY & LAMB STEW

(Khoresht-e Karafs/خورشت کرفس)

*Celery has a very distinct flavor and aroma, and this stew, for those who love celery, is an absolute delight. Lamb meat simmered in a mint, parsley and celery stew is hard to resist. Among green Persian stews, this one is my favorite.*

## SERVES 4

½ cup (50 g) mint

2 cups (120 g) parsley

¾ cup (50 g) celery leaves (optional)

9 oz (250 g) celery

Cooking oil, as needed

1⅔ cups (250 g) finely chopped yellow onions

1 tbsp (9 g) ground turmeric

1 lb (500 g) lamb stew meat (see Note)

Juice of 2 lemons, divided

Salt and pepper, to taste

Persian Plain Rice (page 41) or naan, to serve

Separate the mint and parsley leaves from their thick stems. Wash and dry the leaves, then finely chop and set aside. If your celery has leaves, chop them finely and add to the mint and parsley. Discard the wide part of the celery, then chop each stick into 1-inch (2.5-cm)-long pieces and set aside.

Heat a few tablespoons (30 ml) of oil in a 10-inch (25-cm)-wide pot. Add the onions to the pot, and cook until slightly golden. Add in the turmeric and stir for a minute, then add the lamb and sear until slightly browned, 3 to 4 minutes. Add 4¼ cups (1 L) of water, then cover the pot with a lid, and cook over medium-high heat for 45 minutes to 1 hour. At this stage, the meat will be cooked through but needs more time to be tender.

In a pan, heat a few tablespoons (30 ml) of oil on medium heat. Add the celery and cook until slightly colored—avoid cooking for too long—then remove it from the pan and set aside. In the same pan, add the herbs and cook, stirring occasionally, until the leaves change color and darken a bit. Add more oil if needed. Frying the herbs releases their essence and adds depth to the stew's flavors.

Add the herbs, celery, juice of 1 lemon, salt and pepper to the stew. If the liquid seems too thick, add ⅓ cup (80 ml) of water. Turn the heat to low and let the stew simmer for 15 minutes. Taste the stew and add the juice from the second lemon if desired. Continue cooking over low heat until the meat is tender and the stew has thickened.

Serve the stew with chelo (page 41) or naan.

NOTE

I recommend using 2-inch (5-cm) chunks of lamb leg for the stew meat.

# EGGPLANT, LAMB & TOMATO STEW

## (Khoresht-e Baademjaan/خورشت بادمجان)

*This stew is a beautiful combination of flavors and textures. Tender lamb chunks are cooked in a tomato and sour grape sauce and then paired with creamy fried eggplants. With warm spices and a side of rice, Khoresht-e Baademjaan becomes a true comfort dish.*

### SERVES 4–6

Persian Plain Rice (page 41)

Cooking oil, as needed

1 cup (200 g) finely chopped yellow onions

1¼ lb (1 kg) lamb stew chunks (see Notes)

⅓ cup (75 g) tomato paste

2 tsp (5 g) Stew Mixed Spices (page 22)

1 tbsp (9 g) ground turmeric

½ tsp ground cinnamon

4–6 small, thin eggplants (see Notes)

Salt and pepper, to taste

½ cup (70 g) fresh or frozen unripe sour grapes (see Notes)

4 medium tomatoes, halved

White rice, to serve

Make the rice using the chelo recipe on page 41.

In a medium pot over medium heat, heat a few tablespoons (30 ml) of oil, then cook the onions until golden. Add the lamb and brown for a few minutes. Add the tomato paste, mixed spices, turmeric and cinnamon, and cook for another minute. Add the 3¼ cups (750 ml) of water and bring to a boil, then cover the pot with a lid and cook over medium-low heat for about an hour, until the meat is tender. Check halfway through the cooking time and add more water if needed.

Meanwhile, peel the eggplants, keeping them whole with the green end on. In a pan, heat a few tablespoons (30 ml) of oil on medium heat, then cook the eggplants until golden and soft. Alternatively, you can rub the eggplants with oil and roast them whole in the oven or air fryer.

Once the meat is tender, add salt, pepper and the grapes and stir. Lay the tomatoes and fried eggplants on top and spoon the sauce over everything. Cover the pot with a lid and cook for 15 minutes, until the tomatoes are soft and the eggplants have absorbed the sauce.

Serve the stew with white rice.

> ### NOTES
>
> I recommend using bone-in lamb leg cut into 2-inch (5-cm) chunks for the stew meat.
>
> We use whole eggplants in this stew to keep them from getting soggy in the sauce. It's important to find small, thin eggplants.
>
> Young sour grapes can easily be found in the frozen section of most Middle Eastern stores. You can replace them with ½ cup (120 ml) of verjuice or ¼ cup (60 ml) of lemon juice.

# TAMARIND SPICY FISH STEW

(Qaliyeh Maahi/قلیه ماهی)

*If I were to have only one seafood recipe in this book, it would be Qaliyeh Maahi—a flavorful southern dish with an aromatic tamarind-based sauce and fried fish. It's a healthy dish with a distinct and memorable taste that is easy to prepare.*

## SERVES 2

Persian Plain Rice (page 41, optional)

½ lb (250 g) white fish fillets (any white fish with no bones will work)

Salt and pepper, as needed

1 tsp curry powder

¼ tsp red chili powder (optional)

Cooking oil, as needed

1 cup (200 g) finely chopped yellow onion

1¾ cups (100 g) finely chopped cilantro

1 tsp ground turmeric

1½ tbsp (6 g) dried and crushed fenugreek leaves

1½ tbsp (25 g) tomato paste

⅔ cup (80 g) tamarind paste without seeds (see Note)

1 red or green spicy chile, finely chopped, to garnish (optional)

Cooked rice or bread, to serve

If you'd like to serve this dish with rice, cook the rice using the chelo recipe on page 41.

Wash and dry the fish fillets. If they are too big, you can cut them into 2-inch (5-cm) chunks. Rub both sides of the fillets with salt, pepper, curry powder and red chili powder (if using) and set aside at room temperature to marinate for 10 to 15 minutes.

In a pot, heat a few tablespoons (30 ml) of oil on medium heat, then add the onion and cook until slightly colored. Add the cilantro and cook for 2 to 3 minutes, until the leaves are darkened and wilted. Add in the turmeric, dried fenugreek and tomato paste and stir for another minute over medium heat until the tomato paste turns a dark red. Then add the tamarind paste and 1½ cups (360 ml) water and stir until the paste is dissolved. Cover the pot with a lid and let simmer over low heat for about 15 minutes.

Meanwhile, heat a few tablespoons (30 ml) of oil in a pan over medium heat. Cook the fish fillets until golden.

Taste the sauce and add salt to your liking. If you'd like to keep the fish fillets crispy, skip cooking them further with the sauce and serve the stew with the fish on top. Otherwise, add the fish fillets to the sauce, spoon the sauce over them and cook for another 10 minutes over low heat, until the fish absorbs the sauce. Garnish the stew with chopped chile for extra heat if you wish. Serve with rice or bread.

> NOTE
>
> Tamarind paste is a thick paste with no seeds in it, but some brands sell them with seeds. In that case, you must soak the paste in water and then pass it through a sieve to extract the sauce and remove the seeds. To substitute ⅔ cup (80 g) of seedless paste, mix about 1½ cups (160 g) of tamarind with seeds soaked in 1 cup (240 ml) of water. You will need to reduce the water added to the stew from 1½ cups (360 ml) to ½ cup (120 ml).

# BRAISED LAMB SHANK
## (Maahicheh/ماهیچه)

*Maahicheh is a delicacy served at official ceremonies like weddings but also at home in family gatherings. Older generations believed so much in its magical nutritious power that they would make it for people in recovery from severe sickness or women in postpartum. This dish pairs beautifully with many rice dishes in this book.*

### SERVES 3–4

2½ cups (400 g) yellow onions

Cooking oil, as needed

1¼ lb (1 kg) lamb shank (about 3 pieces)

1 cinnamon stick or 1 tsp ground cinnamon

1½ tsp (5 g) ground turmeric

4 bay leaves

1 tsp whole black peppercorn

⅛ tsp powdered saffron (optional)

Salt, to taste

Preheat the oven to 338°F (170°C). Chop the onions into half-moon shapes and lay them at the bottom of a cast-iron pot or any oven-safe pot big enough to fit the lamb shanks.

In a nonstick pan over high heat, heat a few tablespoons (30 ml) of oil and then cook the lamb shanks until slightly browned. Take the lamb shanks out of the pan and lay them over the onions in the pot. In the pan, add the cinnamon, turmeric, bay leaves and black peppercorn and cook over medium heat. Once the peppercorn starts to pop, add 1 cup (240 ml) water, saffron (if using) and salt, deglaze the pan and then pour the mixture over the lamb shanks in the pot. Cover the pot with the lid and cook in the oven for about 3 hours.

Every hour or so, turn the lamb shanks for an even color and flavor. Check the salt in the last hour of cooking and add more if needed.

Serve with your choice of rice. Maahicheh goes well with Broad Bean and Dill Pilaf (page 71). You can also enjoy the onion mixture as a side or sieve the mixture and use the broth as a sauce.

> NOTE
>
> This dish can also be slow cooked in a pot with a lid on the stovetop instead of in the oven. Make sure to check it every half an hour and add more water if needed.

# CHICKEN IN POMEGRANATE SAUCE

(Khoresht-e Naardoon/خورشت ناردون)

*Khoresht-e Naardoon is a dish from the north of Iran and has the flavor palette of the Caspian shore cities: sweet, sour, garlicky, and it uses pomegranates in different forms. This recipe is easy to prepare with little hands-on work, but it requires patience to cook it slowly and bring all the flavors out. Traditionally, this dish is made with duck that is widely available to the rural community. However, with modern life and the fact that duck meat is an acquired taste, I've replaced it with chicken.*

## SERVES 2–4

2 whole skin-on chicken legs

2 pomegranates (see Note)

Cooking oil, as needed

Salt and pepper, as needed

1 cup (150 g) finely chopped yellow onion

4 cloves garlic, finely chopped

2 tsp (6 g) ground turmeric

3 tbsp (50 g) tomato paste

3½ tbsp (75 g) pomegranate molasses

1 tbsp (13 g) sugar (optional)

Persian Plain Rice (page 41), to serve

### NOTE

Instead of using a whole pomegranate, you can use 2¼ cups (400 g) of pomegranate arils or 1 cup (240 ml) of pomegranate juice.

Wash the chicken legs and pat them dry. If using a whole pomegranate, take the arils out. Set aside 4 tablespoons (44 g) of arils for garnishing, if desired, and juice the rest in a blender with 1 cup (240 ml) water, pulsing a few times. Don't over-blend, to avoid breaking the center seed. Pass the puree through a sieve, discarding the seeds, and set the juice aside.

Heat a few tablespoons (30 ml) of oil in a wide nonstick pan or pot that can fit both chicken legs. Add the chicken legs to the pan, sprinkle them with salt and pepper and cook over medium-high heat until both sides are golden brown. Take the legs out of the pan and set aside.

In the same pan, cook the onion until slightly colored. Add the garlic and stir for a minute until fragrant. Add the turmeric and stir for another minute, then add the tomato paste and mix well. Cook the sauce for another minute or two, until the tomato paste is a darker color. Then add the pomegranate molasses and pomegranate juice and mix. Because different brands of pomegranate molasses will have different levels of sweet and sour, you can taste the sauce and add the sugar if needed.

Add the legs back into the sauce, spoon the sauce over each leg, then cover the pan with a lid and cook over low heat until the legs are tender and the sauce has thickened, 1 to 1½ hours. Check the stew occasionally and spoon the sauce over the chicken.

Take the lid off during the last 10 minutes of cook time to let the sauce thicken if needed.

Drizzle the pomegranate sauce over the chicken to serve. Garnish with more pomegranate arils, if desired, and serve with steamed rice.

# LAMB & BEANS STEW
## (Aabgoosht/آبگوشت)

*Aabgoosht (also called dizi) is one of the oldest traditional Persian recipes widely made across the country with slight variations. It's a comfort food originally made in small individual clay pots cooked for a few hours in the oven. Although you can still see many restaurants in Iran serving it this way, at home they are made in a big pot on the stove.*

### SERVES 4–6

¾ cup (120 g) dry or 2 cups (300 g) canned or cooked chickpeas (see Note)

¾ cup (135 g) dry or 1½ cups (400 g) canned or cooked white beans (see Note)

Vegetable oil, as needed

1⅔ lb (750 g) bone-in lamb or mutton shoulder meat, fat in large chunks (about 4 inches [10 cm] each)

1 large yellow or white onion, quartered

4 medium tomatoes, peeled and quartered

2 tbsp (32 g) tomato paste

2 tbsp (12 g) chopped fresh or dried tarragon

½ tsp ground turmeric

Salt and pepper, to taste

¾ lb (350 g) potatoes

Flatbread and pickled vegetables, to serve

If using dry chickpeas and white beans, soak them in water for at least 8 hours or overnight. Soaking the dry legumes and changing the water a few times helps reduce the bloating effect of the beans.

Heat a few tablespoons (30 ml) of vegetable oil in a large pot over medium heat. Add the meat and cook until slightly brown. Drain the white beans and chickpeas and add them to the pot along with the onion. Add the tomatoes to the pot along with the tomato paste, tarragon, turmeric, salt and pepper. Add 5 cups (1¼ L) water and bring to a boil, then reduce to low and cook for about 2 hours. Check to see if the meat and the legumes are cooked. Add ½ cup (120 ml) of water if the stew is too thick.

Once everything is cooked, wash the potatoes well and add them whole with skins into the pot. Cook for another 30 minutes. Adjust the salt and pepper if needed.

To serve, you can enjoy the stew as is with flatbread and pickled vegetables on the side.

The traditional way of serving this dish is to separate the broth from all the solids and serve it on the side with dried flatbread croutons. The bones are separated from the meat, with the bones and onion being discarded. Everything else is mashed together until smooth. The mash is called *goosht koobideh* and is served with soft flatbread, fresh herbs, *torshi* (pickled vegetables) and a yogurt drink.

---

### NOTE

If using canned legumes, reduce the cooking water from 5 cups (1¼ L) to 4¼ cups (1 L). Add the legumes to the pot after the meat is cooked and at the same time as the potatoes. I recommend using dry legumes, as they become more flavorful while cooking and make the dish a lot more delicious.

# MEATBALLS IN MINT & VINEGAR SAUCE

(Naafeleh Khoozestaani/نافله خوزستانی)

*Meatballs are a common dish all around Iran. Each area has its own version, from orange-sized ones filled with nuts and dried fruits to this southern version from Khuzestaan with small meatballs in mint and onion sauce.*

**SERVES 4**

2 medium yellow onions, grated

1 lb (500 g) ground beef

1 tsp ground turmeric, divided

Salt and pepper, as needed

¾ cup (70 g) + 2 tbsp (12 g) chickpea flour, divided

Vegetable oil, as needed

1½ cups (70 g) Persian-Style Crispy Fried Onions (page 25) or store-bought

3 tbsp (5 g) dried mint

⅓ cup (80 ml) white wine vinegar

2 tbsp (26 g) sugar

White rice or flatbread, to serve

Yogurt, for drizzling (optional)

Squeeze the onions into a colander to remove the excess juice, then mix them together with the beef in a medium-sized bowl. Mix ½ teaspoonof the turmeric, then the salt, pepper and ¾ cup (70 g) of the chickpea flour into the beef and onions. Make walnut-sized meatballs.

Heat a few tablespoons (30 ml) of oil in a nonstick pan. Add the meatballs to the pan and cook over medium heat until all sides are golden. Add the crispy onions, mint, remaining turmeric and pepper to the pan, then stir for a minute. Add the vinegar, 2½ cups (600 ml) water, the sugar, salt and the remaining 2 tablespoons (12 g) of chickpea flour and stir to combine.

Cover the pan with a lid, reduce the heat to low and let the meatballs cook for 10 to 15 minutes while the sauce thickens. Taste the sauce and adjust the salt.

Serve over white steamed rice or with flatbread. Drizzle with some yogurt, if desired, and enjoy.

# In the Bowl

*What is typically known as soup in the West is called* aash *or* aush (آش) *and* shorbaa (شوربا) *in Persian cuisine. However, the word* soup *has entered the Persian vocabulary over the years and is mainly used for any aash with a thin consistency.*

*Aash is a thick soup with herbs and beans as the main ingredients. There are over 400 varieties of aash around the country using local legumes, vegetables, herbs and meat or noodles.*

*In this chapter, I opted not to include any aash recipes for a few reasons. First, the process of making aash can be quite time-consuming as it involves preparing a large quantity of herbs, which can be difficult to purchase in the Western market and can have high prices. Moreover, it requires soaking different kinds of beans overnight and cooking them separately. To maintain the focus of this book as an introduction to Persian cooking, which includes using ingredients and techniques that are easy to find and follow, I decided to omit aash.*

*However, there are still numerous Persian soups that meet the criteria of this book and are unique, delicious and comforting dishes that can be prepared quickly and easily. In this chapter, I have collected a selection of warm and cold soups from different regions of Iran. They are all easy to prepare, have unique flavors and are hearty.*

# BUTTERMILK, WALNUT & TOMATO SOUP
(Kaaljoosh/كالجوش)

*This soup has only a few ingredients but is nutrition packed and high in protein and healthy fat. It's a comforting dish, especially in the cold season. The main component of this soup is kashk, or fermented drained buttermilk. You can read more about it in "Special Ingredients" (page 13). However, in this recipe, I have presented more accessible ingredients to substitute kashk.*

## SERVES 2

¾ cup (90 g) finely chopped walnuts

⅔ lb (300 g) tomatoes

Cooking oil, as needed

⅔ cup (100 g) finely chopped onion

1 tsp ground turmeric

2 tbsp (3 g) dried mint + 1 tsp dried mint, to garnish (optional)

5.6 oz (160 g) fresh kashk (see Notes)

Salt and pepper, to taste

⅓ lb (150 g) goat cheese (optional, see Notes)

2 cups (440 ml) buttermilk (optional, see Notes)

2 tbsp (15 g) toasted and crushed walnuts, to garnish (optional)

1 tbsp (4 g) Persian-Style Crispy Fried Onions (page 25) or store-bought, to garnish (optional)

Thin bread crackers or croutons, to serve

Roast the walnuts in a pan for 2 to 3 minutes, then set aside. Puree the tomatoes with the skin on using a food processor or grater. Heat a few tablespoons (30 ml) of oil in a medium pot over medium heat, then fry the onion until slightly golden. Add the turmeric and dried mint and stir to combine, then continue cooking for another minute, stirring occasionally. Stir in the tomato puree and roasted walnuts and let the mixture simmer.

If using kashk, mix the kashk with 2 cups (480 ml) of water and stir until it dissolves. Add the kashk to the soup and stir well. Let the soup simmer for 10 minutes, then taste and add salt, if needed, and pepper. Add ¼ cup (60 ml) more of water if the soup is too thick. Let the soup simmer for 5 to 10 minutes, then serve.

If using the substitute for kashk, chop the goat cheese into small pieces and add to the pot after adding the tomato puree and walnuts. Stir well until the cheese dissolves, then add the buttermilk. Let it simmer for about 10 minutes, then add salt and pepper to taste. If it's too thick, add ¼ cup (60 ml) of water and simmer for another 10 minutes, then serve.

You can garnish this dish with extra toasted walnuts, crispy onions and mint-infused oil. To make infused oil, heat 2 tablespoons (30 ml) of oil in a small pan. Once hot, add 1 teaspoon of dried mint and stir. Cook for about a minute, then immediately remove the pan from the heat and pour the oil into a small cup to avoid further cooking. Garnish your soup with the oil and serve with thin bread crackers or croutons.

> NOTES
>
> Kashk is salty, so it's essential to not add salt before adding the kashk. Taste the food after adding the kashk and add salt if needed.
>
> If you'd like to substitute the kashk, use the goat cheese and buttermilk.

# BEAN & TOMATO STEW
(Khoraak-e Loobiaa/خوراک لوبیا)

*Bean stew is a typical dish in many cultures. It's comforting and nutritious, especially on cold days. Here is the Persian version of this ancient dish. This stew is enjoyed on its own with some bread or served as a side with other dishes like Omelete Shaapoori (page 112). You can use either pinto or white beans depending on your preference.*

## SERVES 4

1⅓ cups (250 g) dry pinto or white beans or 3 cups (500 g) shelled fresh beans

Cooking oil, as needed

1 cup (150 g) finely chopped yellow onion

1 tsp ground turmeric powder

2 tsp (4 g) curry powder

3 tbsp (50 g) tomato paste

1 medium tomato, peeled and chopped

2 cloves garlic, finely chopped

1 medium potato, peeled and quartered

Salt and pepper, to taste

Juice of 2 bitter oranges or 1 lemon

1 tsp powdered Persian hogweed, to garnish (optional)

1 tsp chili flakes, to garnish (optional)

If using dry beans, wash and soak them in water for 10 to 12 hours or overnight. If possible, change the water a couple of times during the soaking time. Soaking for long hours not only shortens the cooking time but also makes the beans easier to digest and reduces bloating.

Drain the beans after soaking and cook them in a medium-sized pot with 3¼ cups (750 ml) of water until cooked through, 30 to 45 minutes. If using fresh beans, you can skip the soaking time and cook them directly.

Heat a few tablespoons (30 ml) of oil in a pan and fry the onion until slightly colored. Add the turmeric, curry powder and tomato paste, then stir for a minute until the tomato paste turns darker in color. Add the tomato and garlic and cook for 2 to 3 minutes over medium heat, stirring occasionally, then turn off the heat and set the pan aside.

Once the beans are cooked, add the tomato and onion sauce to a pot with the potato. Cook on low for 15 minutes. Once the potato is cooked, remove from the pot and mash with a fork. Add the potato back to the pot. Stir in salt and pepper to taste and let the stew simmer for another 10 minutes.

Before serving, add in the bitter orange juice and stir well. Serve with a dash of powdered Persian hogweed and chili flakes to garnish, if desired.

# SPICY RED LENTIL DAAL

## (Daal Adas-e Booshehri/دال عدس بوشهری)

*Daal is a soup originating from the southern provinces of Iran by the Persian Gulf. It's a simple dish that is quick to make but full of flavor. Daal is usually served with bread, but a thicker version also goes with rice.*

### SERVES 4

1½ cups (270 g) red lentils

¾ cup (125 g) tamarind pulp with seeds or 2 tbsp (15 g) tamarind paste with no seeds

Cooking oil, as needed

1 cup (150 g) finely chopped onion

4 cloves garlic, finely chopped

1 tbsp (9 g) ground turmeric

¼ tsp ground cayenne red pepper

2 tbsp (13 g) hot or mild curry powder, divided

⅔ lb (300 g) potatoes, peeled and cubed

Salt and pepper, to taste

¼ cup (15 g) chopped cilantro, to garnish (optional)

1 tbsp (7 g) chili flakes, to garnish (optional)

Wash the lentils a few times and set them aside. If using tamarind pulp with seeds, soak the pulp in 1 cup (240 ml) of water.

Heat a large pot and add a few tablespoons (30 ml) of cooking oil, then fry the onion over medium heat until golden. Add the garlic and stir. Mix in the turmeric, cayenne red pepper and half of the curry powder. Stir for a minute, then add the potatoes and lentils and cook for another minute. Sieve the tamarind, discard the seeds and add the sauce to the pot. If using tamarind paste without seeds, mix with 1 cup (240 ml) of water and add it to the pot. Add 3 more cups (720 ml) of water to the pot and bring to a boil. Cover with a lid and let the soup cook over medium heat until the lentils and potatoes are soft. If the daal is too thick, add ½ cup (120 ml) of water. Add salt and pepper and stir well.

Before serving, heat 1 tablespoon (15 ml) of oil and add the remaining curry powder. Let the oil sizzle until fragrant. Drizzle the soup with the curry oil and garnish with the cilantro and chili flakes if desired.

# BARLEY & CILANTRO SOUP

(Soup-e Jo va Geshniz-e Tabrizi/سوپ جو و گشنیز تبریزی)

*Barley soups are a favorite in many cuisines. In Persian cuisine, different regions have their own take on barley soup. This version from Tabriz, the Azari region of Iran, is one of my favorites. It's rich, creamy and flavorful, making it an excellent comfort food.*

## SERVES 4

¾ cup (150 g) thick-rolled barley or oats

1 cup (60 g) finely chopped cilantro, divided

Cooking oil, as needed

1 small yellow onion, finely chopped

4¼ cups (1 L) chicken broth, vegetable broth or a mix of both (see Note)

1 cup (100 g) peeled and grated carrots

1 clove garlic, grated

2 cups (500 ml) buttermilk

¼ cup (60 g) full-fat yogurt

Salt and pepper, to taste

Olive oil, as needed (optional)

Paprika or ground cayenne red pepper (optional)

Persian-Style Crispy Fried Onions (page 25) or store-bought, to garnish (optional)

Wash the barley and soak it in a bowl with water. Set aside 3 tablespoons (11 g) of the cilantro for garnish.

In a large pot, fry the onion with a few tablespoons (30 ml) of oil for 2 to 3 minutes over medium heat—no need to fry until golden. Drain the soaked barley and add it to the pot along with the chicken broth. Cook for 10 to 15 minutes, until the grains are soft. Add the carrots and cook for 5 minutes, then add the garlic and remaining cilantro and cook for 4 to 5 more minutes. Add the buttermilk and yogurt while stirring constantly to avoid the dairy from separating. Taste the soup and add salt and pepper if needed, then cook on low for another 10 minutes.

Optional: Heat a few tablespoons (30 ml) of olive oil, then add the paprika and stir. Turn the heat off and let the oil sit for a couple of minutes.

Garnish the soup with the infused oil, chopped cilantro and crispy onions if desired.

> NOTE
>
> If you like to use powdered or tablet broth concentrates, use 2 to 3 tablets or 2 to 3 tablespoons (13 to 20 g) of broth powder in 4¼ cups (1 L) of water. Different kinds of broth concentrate have different amounts of salt; start with two broth concentrate cubes or two tablespoons of broth concentrate powder first and add more later if needed.

# COLD YOGURT SOUP WITH FRESH HERBS & NUTS

### (Aab-Doogh Khiyaar/آبدوغ خیار)

*This dish is the ultimate superfood, a balanced and nutritious cold soup perfect for fighting the heat. It's a complete meal with protein, carbs, healthy fat, fiber and vitamins with subtle and balanced flavors. There are some sayings that this dish comes from the famous city of Shiraz, but despite the uncertain origin, it's a popular soup prepared across the country in the summer season.*

## SERVES 3–4

⅔ cup (100 g) raisins

8.8 oz (250 g) cucumber

1¾ cups (500 g) Greek yogurt

6 radishes, thinly sliced

¼ cup (15 g) finely chopped parsley

¼ cup (10 g) finely chopped basil

1 tbsp (10 g) finely chopped fresh tarragon or 1½ tbsp (5 g) dried tarragon

1 tbsp (2 g) dried mint or 2 tbsp (11 g) finely chopped fresh mint

1 green onion, finely chopped

½ cup (60 g) finely chopped walnuts

1 tbsp (1 g) crushed dried rose petals (optional)

Salt and pepper, to taste

1½ cups (326 g) ice cubes

Thin bread crackers or croutons, for serving

Wash the raisins and soak them in a cup with water while you prepare the rest of the ingredients. If using long regular cucumbers, cut the cucumber lengthwise and scoop the seeds out with a spoon. Chop the cucumber into small cubes.

In a large mixing bowl, mix the yogurt and 1¼ cups (300 ml) cold water. Drain the raisins and add them along with the cucumber, radishes, parsley, basil, tarragon, mint and green onion to the bowl. Add the walnuts, rose petals (if using) and salt and pepper, and stir to combine.

Add the ice cubes to the bowl and serve right away. Enjoy with bread crackers or croutons.

# Breakfast & Brunch

*A typical breakfast in Persian culture includes flatbread, butter, cheese, walnuts, pistachios, clotted cream, honey and seasonal jam, served with a hot cup of black tea. For a heartier breakfast, omelets, porridge-like bowls and meat- or legume-based soups are also popular.*

*Certain dishes such as* halim *(a porridge made with wheat and turkey) and* kaleh paacheh *(a soup made with lamb face meat) need to be slowly cooked overnight and require a lot of preparation time. As a result, these dishes are typically served early in the morning at specific diners instead of being prepared at home.*

*Within this chapter, we will explore a variety of well-known dishes originating from various regions that come together in no time.*

# BUTTERNUT SQUASH PATTIES
## (Kouyi Kaakaa/کویی کاکاا)

*Kouyi Kaakaa is an Iranian dish from Gilan in the northern province of Iran by the Caspian Sea. If I want to translate it to a Western dish, it would be a sweet squash pancake with beautiful autumnal flavors. Traditionally, it's made sweeter, sprinkled with powdered sugar and served with tea. In this recipe, I reduced the amount of sugar so it could be served with maple syrup on the side.*

### YIELDS 12 PANCAKES

2 cups (280 g) peeled and cubed butternut squash

7 tbsp (100 ml) milk

1 large egg

1 cup (120 g) all-purpose flour

1 tbsp (15 ml) rose water

1 tsp ground cinnamon

½ tsp ground cardamom

2 tbsp (30 g) sugar

1 tsp baking powder

¼ tsp salt

Cooking oil, as needed

Maple syrup, to serve (see Note)

2 tbsp (30 g) butter, to serve (optional)

In a large pot, add the butternut squash and enough water to cover the pieces. Cook until the squash is soft, 15 to 20 minutes. Drain the water out, move the cooked squash to a large bowl and mash well until smooth. Let it cool.

Add the milk and egg to the mashed squash and whisk together. Then add the flour, rose water, cinnamon, cardamom, sugar, baking powder and salt and mix until incorporated. Let the mixture rest for 15 to 20 minutes.

Add a few tablespoons (30 ml) of oil to a nonstick pan over medium heat and make the pancakes, using 2 to 3 tablespoons (15 to 30 ml) of batter per pancake. This batter needs oil to cook beautifully, so add more as needed. Fry each side of the pancakes until golden.

Serve the pancakes with a side of maple syrup. To make a more delicious and rich syrup, you can melt the butter and mix it with some maple syrup before pouring the mixture over the pancakes.

> NOTE
>
> As butternut squash varies in sweetness, you can control how sweet the pancakes are with your syrup at the end. I recommend you first try one without maple syrup, then add the syrup as desired.

# SPINACH ONION OMELET

## (Nargessi/نرگسی)

*Nargessi means "like narcissus," the flower, a beautiful annotation of this dish's appearance. Although simple, the ingredients and the way they pair together create magic.*

### SERVES 4

⅛ tsp powdered saffron (optional)

4 tbsp (60 ml) cold water (optional)

Cooking oil, as needed

2 small yellow onions, halved and thinly sliced

2 cloves garlic, grated

½ tsp ground turmeric

7 oz (200 g) baby spinach

Salt and pepper, to taste

4 large eggs

Juice of 1 bitter orange or juice of ½ orange and ½ lemon

Bread, to serve

If using the saffron, in a small bowl, mix the saffron with the cold water and set aside to brew.

Heat a few tablespoons (30 ml) of oil in a nonstick pan over medium heat, then cook the onions, stirring occasionally, until evenly fried and golden. Add the garlic and stir a minute until fragrant. Then add the turmeric and stir until warm and well mixed. Remove the mixture from the pan and set aside. Wilt the spinach in the same pan until soft and well cooked, then season with salt and pepper. Add the onions back to the pan and stir to combine.

Make four nests in the mixture and break the eggs into them. Season the eggs with salt and pepper. Put the lid on and cook on low until the egg white is cooked and the yolk is to your liking.

Before serving, drizzle with the brewed saffron and bitter orange juice. Serve with a side of bread.

> ### NOTE
>
> Finding bitter oranges can be tricky all year round, but they have such an excellent acidic taste that I highly recommend using them if you find them. To substitute, mix half a portion of orange juice and lemon juice plus the zest of half a lemon.

# FRIED CHEESE OMELET

### (Panir Bereshteh/پنیر برشته)

*Panir Bereshteh is one of my favorite breakfasts to make. This dish is from northern Iran and has the typical flavors of garlic and herbs from that area. The fried cheese adds an irresistible richness to this humble dish.*

### SERVES 4

3 tbsp (42 g) butter

1 tbsp (15 ml) olive oil

4 small cloves garlic, grated

2 tsp (6 g) ground turmeric

2 tbsp (6 g) dried dill

14 oz (400 g) feta cheese, crumbled (see Notes)

4 large eggs

1 tbsp (1 g) fresh dill, to garnish (optional)

Toast or flatbread, to serve

Melt the butter in a nonstick pan over medium heat, then add the olive oil. Add the garlic, turmeric and dried dill and stir for a minute until the garlic becomes slightly golden and fragrant. Then add the feta cheese and cook for 2 to 3 minutes.

Break the eggs into a bowl and briefly whisk. The cheese will begin to release water; once the water has evaporated and the cheese is slightly golden, add the eggs to the cheese. Stir together and let it cook.

Once the eggs are set, the omelet is ready. Sprinkle with fresh dill and enjoy on toast or with flatbread.

### NOTES

We don't add salt to this dish as feta cheese is usually salty. I recommend tasting your feta cheese first, and if it is too salty, wash the block of cheese with cold water and dry it with a kitchen towel. If using unsalted cheese, season with salt to your liking while cooking. You can also use cottage cheese for this recipe.

A simple version of this omelet I make often skips both the dill and garlic. The fried feta with butter and egg still makes an irresistible breakfast.

# TOMATO PASTE OMELET WITH BEANS

(Omelete Shaapoori/املت شاپوری)

*This omelet gets its name from a small café owner in Rasht, the capital of Gilan province in the north of Iran. It's a delicious combination of white or pinto beans in a tomato sauce omelet topped with bitter orange juice and Persian hogweed! If you have a favorite canned bean, feel free to use them instead of the homemade version for a quick preparation.*

## SERVES 2

3 tbsp (42 g) butter or vegetable oil

3 tbsp (50 g) tomato paste

½ tsp ground turmeric

4 large eggs

Salt and pepper, as needed

Bean and Tomato Stew (page 96)

Juice of 1 bitter orange or juice of ½ orange and ½ lemon (see Note)

¼ tsp Persian hogweed powder (optional)

In a large nonstick pan, melt the butter, then add the tomato paste and turmeric and cook for a minute, stirring often. When the tomato paste becomes darker in color, add ⅓ cup (80 ml) water and mix until a sauce is formed. Add in the eggs, salt and pepper to the sauce and stir.

Push the omelet to one half of the pan and add the bean stew to the other half. Cook until the eggs have become firm and the bean stew is warm.

To serve, drizzle the bitter-orange juice on the bean stew. Serve the omelet with the bean stew on the side and sprinkle with Persian hogweed powder if desired.

> **NOTE**
>
> Bitter oranges are hard to find when not in season, but an equal amount of orange juice and lemon juice with some lemon peel zest has a very similar taste.

# DATE, WALNUT & SESAME OMELET
## (Qisaavaa/قیساوا)

*This omelet from the Azari region of Iran is perfect for cold days. It's sweet with a gentle cardamom and cinnamon aroma and nutty toasted walnut flavor. It is nutrition packed and hearty and keeps you full for a long time.*

### SERVES 2–3

8–9 pitted dates

4 large eggs

2 tbsp (28 g) butter

¼ cup (30 g) chopped walnuts

½ tsp ground cinnamon

¼ tsp ground cardamom

½ tsp white sesame seed

Bread, to serve

If the dates are hard, put them in a bowl with ⅓ cup (80 ml) of hot water and let them soak for 10 to 15 minutes. Break the eggs in a cup and whisk well until slightly bubbly.

Once the dates are soft, add the butter to a pan over medium-low heat and toast the walnuts with the dates for a minute. Add the cinnamon and cardamon and stir for a minute. Add the whisked eggs to the pan and sprinkle with the sesame seeds. Cook the eggs until firm.

Serve the omelet with a side of bread.

# CLOTTED CREAM

## (Sarshir/سرشیر)

*Freshly toasted bread and thick, lush clotted cream with honey were among my favorite breakfasts as a child. While growing up, there were still many traditional dairy shops around town—stores were not yet filled with packaged factory products. Every time we craved fresh clotted cream, my dad could buy it quickly from one of those farm-to-market shops close to us. Later though, as these little local shops lost their business to bigger chain stores and finding fresh clotted cream became harder, I was determined to learn to make it myself. To my surprise, the homemade version of sarshir was as good as those of local shops and relatively simple to make with some patience.*

**SERVES 4–6**

1 cup (220 ml) full-fat milk

3 cups (700 ml) 33% fat cream

Toast, scones or flatbread, to serve (optional)

Jam, to serve (optional)

Honey, crushed nuts or rose petals, to garnish (optional)

Fill a large pot with water to the top, leaving 2 to 3 inches (5 to 7.5 cm) empty, and bring the water to a boil. In another pot, warm the milk, turning off the heat before it boils. Add the cream and stir to combine.

Choose a heat-resistant dish that is not metal or plastic and is big enough to fit on top of the pot to use for a bain-marie. Add the warm cream mixture to the heat-resistant dish and place it on top of the boiling pot. Reduce the heat to low and let the cream simmer for 4 to 10 hours. You need a minimum of 4 hours for the cream to form, but cooking it longer creates thicker clotted cream. I usually leave it to cook overnight.

At this point, you should see a thick yellow skin that has formed on the top with the liquid underneath. Leaving the skin on, place the dish in the fridge for 8 to 24 hours. Then, lifting the thick cream from one corner of the container, empty the liquid under it into a cup. You can use the liquid for baking or discard it.

Release the cream from the dish completely using the tip of a knife. Flip it onto a large piece of parchment paper and start rolling it over itself. Keep the rolled clotted cream in the fridge in an airtight container.

You can serve the clotted cream with toast or scones and your choice of jam. I like to drizzle it with honey, sprinkle with crushed nuts and rose petals and serve with fresh flatbread.

# QUINCE JAM

## (Morabbaa-ye- Beh/مربای به)

*Quinces in Persian are called* beh, *which also means* nice, *and there might be a direct connection between our love for this fruit and its name. Quince has a texture between a hard pear and an apple but is not as juicy. What makes them so desirable is how fragrant they are, and once you cook them, they turn from pale yellow to a stunning ruby color. Iranians use quinces in cooking, with the jam being a favorite, but I also find them fantastic in pies.*

### YIELDS 2 CUPS (580 G)

3 quinces, peeled and chopped

Quince seeds (optional)

1⅔ cups (330 g) sugar

8 cardamom pods

The edible seeds from the quinces can naturally thicken the jam syrup, so set aside the seeds if desired.

Add the sugar and 2 cups (450 ml) water to a pot and stir until it dissolves. Add the quinces and their seeds to the pot. Crack the cardamom pods with the tip of a knife and add them to the rest of the ingredients. Cover the pot with a lid and bring to a boil, then reduce the heat and cook for 3 to 4 hours. Every hour or so, gently stir the quinces. Once they are ruby red, the jam is ready.

If your syrup looks too runny, cook without the lid over medium heat for another 10 to 15 minutes, until it thickens. Let it cool, then discard the cardamom pods and store the jam in a clean airtight jar. Quince Jam is delicious with butter and toast or on clotted cream, yogurt or granola. It also goes great on a cheese platter.

> **NOTES**
>
> The secret to getting the ruby color is to cook with the lid closed and over low heat for a long time. To avoid having mushy fruit, try to be gentle when stirring and avoid stirring too many times.
>
> The syrup gets thicker once the jam has cooled down, so be mindful not to make the jam too dry by overcooking it.

# Something to Share

As mentioned in the introduction (page 10), a typical Persian table consists of a main dish accompanied by some smaller dishes to share, condiments and appetizers, all in shared portions. Many of the dishes served as small dishes in gatherings are often themselves a complete meal.

This chapter will introduce you to some of the most renowned and delicious sharing dishes from various regions. These dishes can be used as the main course or served as finger food or a side dish at parties. For instance, kuku, a traditional Persian fritter, is a versatile dish that can be transformed into a tasty sandwich or served as a side dish. Please note that the portions mentioned in this chapter are intended for sharing or as side dishes.

# LETTUCE & DILL PATTIES

(Kookoo Kaahoo Shevid/کوکوی کاهو شوید)

*If you enjoy Iranian food, you may have heard about the famous Persian herb patties kuku sabzi. This dish is a simplified version of it. This kuku only has three herbs and comes together quickly, but when it comes to taste, it does not fall short of its fancier version. We usually serve it with bread, tomatoes and pickles. It makes a deliciously healthy sandwich.*

## SERVES 3–6

½ lb (250 g) fresh dill

⅔ cup (30 g) chives

150 g romaine lettuce

6 eggs

¼ tsp ground turmeric

¼ tsp ground cinnamon

Salt and pepper, to taste

1 tbsp (8 g) all-purpose flour

Cooking oil, as needed

Bread, tomatoes, pickles and your favorite sauce, to serve

Start by washing the dill, chives and lettuce, and pat them dry. Next, discard any long and thick stems and finely chop the leaves. You can also use a food processor, but a board and knife are preferred. A food processor can crush the herbs and make them soggy, affecting the patties' texture.

Add the herbs and lettuce to a large mixing bowl. Break the eggs in another bowl and whisk until thoroughly mixed and slightly foamy. Next, add the turmeric, cinnamon, salt, pepper and flour to the eggs and mix well. Add the egg mixture to the herbs and lettuce and stir to combine.

You can fry the patties in different ways. You can use a large pan to heat some oil, then pour in the patty mixture. Cover with a lid and cook on low until the center is set. Then cut the cooked patty into small pieces, turn over and fry the other side.

Another way is to spoon small amounts of the mixture into a hot pan with oil to make smaller individual patties.

You can also use round cookie cutters. Put them in the hot pan, add oil and spoon the mixture into the cookie cutters. Fry on low, and once the center is set, release the patties, turn them over and cook the other side.

Once the patties are cooked through, set them on a kitchen towel to absorb the excess oil and cool down. Serve the patties with bread, tomatoes and pickles. Drizzle with your go-to sauce.

# SPICY SHRIMP & POTATOES

## (Dopiyaazeh Meygoo/دوپیازه میگو)

*Dopiyaazeh translates as "two onions," a meat and onion–based food popular in the south and east of Iran, Afghanistan, India and Pakistan. Here I am sharing the shrimp version with you. This dish is loved and made by coastal cities in the south like Bushahr, Qeshm and Bandar Abbas, where freshly caught seafood is abundantly available.*

### SERVES 2–4

1½ tbsp (10 g) mild curry powder

½ tsp harissa powder

1 tsp paprika

⅔ lb (300 g) raw shrimp, cleaned, peeled and tail removed

⅔ lb (300 g) potatoes, peeled and cut into ½" (1.3-cm) cubes

Cooking oil, as needed

1¾ cups (200 g) yellow onions, halved and thinly sliced

1 tsp ground turmeric

2 tbsp (35 g) tomato paste

4–5 cloves garlic, finely chopped

1 dried lime (optional)

Salt and pepper, to taste

3 tbsp (10 g) cilantro

1 red chile, chopped (optional)

1 lime, cut into wedges

Flatbread or rice, to serve

In a mixing bowl, combine the curry powder, harissa powder and paprika. Add the shrimp and toss until coated with the spices, then set aside to marinate.

The potatoes can either be cooked in a pan with some oil on the stovetop or tossed with a little bit of oil and roasted in the oven until golden. Set the cooked potatoes aside.

In a large pan, heat a few tablespoons (30 ml) of oil. Cook the onions over medium heat until caramelized and golden. Add the turmeric and stir for a minute. Add the shrimp with the spices to the pan, then cook over medium-high heat until the shrimp is pink and cooked through. Do not overcook the shrimp; about 2 minutes on each side is enough. Add the tomato paste and garlic and cook for 1 to 2 minutes, until it turns darker in color.

Cut the dried lime (if using), separate the brown pieces inside from the skin and discard the skin. Finely chop the brown pieces and add them to the pan. Add ⅓ cup (80 ml) of water to the pan along with the cooked potatoes. Add salt and pepper, mix well and cook for 1 to 2 minutes. Remove from the heat to stop cooking.

To serve, sprinkle torn cilantro and the chopped chile (if using) on top and set the lime wedges on the side. This dish can be served with either flatbread or rice.

# SMOKY EGGPLANT & WALNUT DIP

(Kaal Kabaab/کال کباب)

*This dish is another flavor-packed recipe from the north of Iran. The smoky eggplants pair perfectly with fragrant fresh herbs, sweet and sour pomegranate and rich, nutty walnuts. Kaal Kabaab is a side dish to enjoy on its own or as an appetizer with other meals.*

SERVES 4–8

6 medium eggplants

1 cup (130 g) walnuts

¼ cup (20 g) chopped cilantro

2 tbsp (10 g) chopped mint

3 tbsp (10 g) chopped fresh oregano

1¾ cups (300 g) pomegranate arils, divided

3–4 cloves garlic, grated

1 tbsp (21 g) pomegranate molasses

Salt and pepper, to taste

To cook the eggplants, grill them whole, skin on, on a charcoal grill until the insides are soft to the touch and the skins are charred. Using a grill to roast the eggplants is the preferred method, as it creates the deep smoky flavor we are looking for in this recipe. For alternative methods, refer to the Notes.

Once the eggplants are cooked, put them in a tray and cover for about 10 minutes. Then remove the skin, mash the flesh and set aside in a bowl.

Grind the walnuts in a food processor until a soft paste forms, then add to a large mixing bowl along with the herbs. Set aside ½ cup (100 g) of the pomegranate arils and blend the rest in the food processor until only the seeds and juice have separated. Pass the liquid through a sieve and add to the bowl with the other ingredients. Add the garlic, pomegranate molasses, salt and pepper, and stir until a paste forms. Then add the mashed eggplants and mix well. If the mixture has a lumpy texture, blend it with a stick blender or pulse it a few times in the food processor.

Let the dip rest for a few hours in the fridge to enhance the flavors, but you can also serve it immediately. Garnish with the reserved pomegranate arils to serve.

## NOTES

Alternatively, you can cook the eggplants in the oven or an air fryer. Preheat the oven to 390°F (200°C). Lay the eggplants whole on a tray covered with parchment paper and cook under the grill until they are cooked through and have slightly charred skin, about 15 minutes. Be careful not to overcook as the flesh can get dry.

You can char the skin with a kitchen torch once the eggplants are cooked to give them a smoky flavor. Let them cool down, covered, for about 10 minutes before peeling the skin and mashing the flesh.

# MEAT & POTATO PATTIES

## (Kotlet/کتلت)

*Kotlet must be one of the most loved childhood foods in my country. If you ask any Iranian about kotlet, there is a high chance they say that their mothers would make the best ones! These patties check all the criteria of a memorable comfort food. The potatoes, meat and spices are blended together and fried until golden and crispy on the outside but soft inside. The smell of them cooking is so appetizing that half the portion is usually eaten right at the stovetop!*

## SERVES 4–8

1½ lb (700 g) russet potatoes

1¼ cups (200 g) finely grated onions

1 lb (500 g) ground beef

1 tbsp (10 g) ground turmeric

1 tsp paprika

1 tsp ground coriander

1 tbsp (18 g) salt

½ tsp ground black pepper

1½ tsp (4 g) ground cinnamon

2 eggs

2 tbsp (14 g) breadcrumbs

Cooking oil, as needed

Flatbread or pita, to serve

Your favorite toppings, to serve

Boil the potatoes until fully cooked. Let them cool completely, then peel and grate them with the bigger side of a grater (see Note). Squeeze the grated onions in a colander to remove the excess juice, then add them to a large bowl with the potatoes. Add the ground beef, turmeric, paprika, coriander, salt, pepper and cinnamon to the bowl and mix until all the ingredients are well incorporated. Add the eggs one at a time and mix well. If you have time, let the mixture rest in the fridge for about 1 hour. Right before cooking, add the breadcrumbs and give it all a good mix with your hands.

Take a small amount of the meat-and-potato mixture, about the size of a tangerine, and make a flat disk. Heat the oil in a pan over medium heat, then add the patties. Once one side is golden brown, flip the patties over and fry the other side. Rest the patties on a plate with a kitchen towel under them to absorb any excess oil.

Enjoy the kotlet with flatbread or pita and your favorite toppings, such as tomatoes, pickles, fresh herbs like cilantro and coriander, feta cheese, yogurt sauce or olives.

> NOTE
>
> It's essential to let the potatoes cool down completely. If the potatoes are too warm, they will mash instead of grate, which will make the patties dense.

# TABRIZI STUFFED EGGPLANT

### (Gaarni Yaarikh/گارنی یاریخ)

*This is a dish from the Turkish provinces in Iran. Azari people are famous for their appetizing food. Gaarni Yaarikh translates to "open belly," which refers to the eggplants being opened and filled with a thick, aromatic meat sauce. This dish can be served as a meal or a side to share.*

SERVES 4–8

## EGGPLANT

4 large eggplants

Salt, as needed

Cooking oil, as needed

1.4 oz (40 g) dried barberries or ½ cup (50 g) dried cranberries

1 cup (200 g) finely chopped yellow onion

14 oz (400 g) ground beef

1 tbsp (9 g) ground turmeric

1½ tsp (4 g) mild curry powder

½ tsp ground black pepper

¼ cup (65 g) tomato paste

2 cups (350 g) tomatoes, peeled and chopped

3 green onions, chopped

4 cloves garlic, grated

1 red chile, chopped, divided

½ cup (30 g) chopped fresh parsley

## TOMATO SAUCE

Cooking oil, as needed

¼ cup (65 g) tomato paste

1 tsp mild curry powder

½ tsp garlic powder

½ tsp onion powder

Pinch of salt

2½ tbsp (38 ml) white wine vinegar

1 tbsp (13 g) sugar

Wash the eggplants, then peel the skin in alternating stripes: one strip peeled, one strip unpeeled. Don't cut the ends off. Rub the eggplants with salt and let them sit for about 30 minutes.

Preheat the oven to 410°F (210°C). (Alternatively, you can fry the eggplants on the stove, but it will require more oil.) After 30 minutes, rinse the eggplants, dry them, then rub them all over with oil. Lay the eggplants on a baking dish lined with parchment paper and bake for about 15 minutes, until golden. Set them aside to cool down. If using barberries, wash them and soak them in water for about 15 minutes, then drain the water and set aside.

In a pan, fry the onion with a few tablespoons (30 ml) of oil until golden. Add the ground beef and cook until slightly browned. Then add the turmeric, curry powder, salt and pepper and stir for a minute. Stir in the tomato paste and fry for another minute. Add the tomatoes, green onions, garlic, barberries and half of the chile and cook for another minute. Mix in ½ cup (120 ml) water, then simmer on low until the sauce thickens, 4 to 5 minutes.

Create a vertical cut in the center of the eggplants without cutting all the way through. Try to make the cut wider with a spoon. If there are seeds, you can scoop them out. Divide the meat sauce between the eggplants, making each one full enough that it overflows slightly.

To make the tomato sauce, in a pan big enough to lay all 4 eggplants, add a few tablespoons (30 ml) of oil over medium heat and cook the tomato paste for 1 minute. Stir in the curry powder, garlic powder and onion powder and cook for another minute, scraping the bottom of the pan with your spatula to avoid burning the paste. Add 1½ cups (360 ml) water, salt, vinegar and sugar, and stir well. Bring to a boil, then reduce the heat to low. Gently lay the eggplants in the sauce, then cover the pan with a lid and cook for 15 to 20 minutes, until the sauce thickens and the eggplants are cooked.

To serve, spread a few spoonfuls of sauce on each plate, then lay an eggplant on top. Garnish with the parsley and reserved chile.

# SMOKY EGGPLANT & TOMATO SPREAD

## (Mirzaa Qaasemi/میرزا قاسمی)

*Mirzaa Qaasemi has a special place in my heart. It's a recipe from the north of Iran, where my mom is from. The dishes of this region are flavorful because of the use of garlic and many wild herbs. Mirzaa Qaasemi can be considered a spread or dip. It's a creamy, smoky and savory dish enjoyed with flatbread or white rice.*

*I have vivid memories of my mother cooking it. Without an open space for a fire to barbecue, my mom would put the eggplants directly on our gas stove. I remember standing there with my eyes on the same level as the stovetop, looking at the eggplants' skin brightening up with the flames and turning red, then gray into ashes. The scene was mesmerizing and the smell was amazing.*

### SERVES 4–8

6 medium eggplants

5–6 tomatoes, peeled and roughly chopped, or 4 cups (1 kg) canned chopped tomatoes

Salt and pepper, to taste

Cooking oil, as needed

1 bulb garlic, cloves grated

1 tbsp (16 g) tomato paste

1½ tsp (5 g) ground turmeric

4 large eggs

To cook the eggplants, grill them whole, skin on, on a charcoal grill. Cook them until the inside is soft to the touch and the skin is charred. Using a grill to roast the eggplants is the preferred method as it creates the deep smoky flavor we are looking for in this recipe. For alternative methods, refer to the Note.

Once the eggplants are roasted, put them in a tray and cover for 10 minutes. Then remove the skin, mash the flesh and set aside.

Add the tomatoes to a pan over medium heat and cook, stirring occasionally, until the tomatoes become a thick sauce, then add the salt, pepper and a few tablespoons (30 ml) of oil. Stir, then make a well in the center. Add another tablespoon (15 ml) of oil in the center, then add the garlic and cook for about a minute. Stir the tomato paste and turmeric with the garlic and cook for a few minutes. Once the paste begins changing color, mix everything in the pan together. Add the eggplants, stir all the ingredients well and cook for about 5 minutes, until everything is incorporated and a paste forms.

Make a well in the center again and add 1 tablespoon (15 ml) of oil. Break the eggs in the hole and stir to scramble. Once the egg is cooked, mix all the ingredients together. Serve warm.

> ### NOTE
>
> Alternatively, cook the eggplants in the oven or an air fryer. Preheat the oven to 390°F (200°C). Lay the eggplants whole on a tray covered with parchment paper and cook under the grill until they are cooked through and have slightly charred skin, about 15 minutes.

# EGGPLANT & BUTTERMILK SPREAD

(Kashk-e Baademjaan/کشک بادمجان)

*Kashk-e baademjaan is a beloved appetizer, cherished by many Iranian and non-Iranians, and if you try it once, you'll know why. The creamy eggplant with crunchy walnut chunks paired with caramelized onion and garlic makes a unique dish hard to pass up. It also has kashk (page 13), a fermented, salted buttermilk paste that adds a layer of umami to the whole plate.*

### SERVES 4–8

5 medium eggplants, peeled and quartered

Cooking oil, as needed

Salt, as needed

1 medium yellow onion, finely chopped

1 tbsp (9 g) ground turmeric

Black pepper, to taste

7 tbsp (50 g) finely chopped walnuts

4 cloves garlic, finely chopped

2 tbsp (3 g) dried mint

2.8 oz (80 g) fresh kashk or ¼ lb (100 g) goat cheese (see Notes)

½ cup (30 g) Persian-Style Crispy Fried Onions (page 25) or store-bought, to garnish (optional)

2 tbsp (10 g) crispy garlic, to garnish (optional)

Flatbread, to serve

Preheat the oven to 375°F (190°C). Rub the eggplants with oil and a pinch of salt. Lay them in a baking tray lined with parchment paper. Roast the eggplants until golden. Remove the tray from the oven and mash the eggplants. Alternatively, you can cook the eggplants whole with skin on in the oven until cooked through, then cut and scoop out the flesh and mash.

In a nonstick pan over medium heat, add a few tablespoons (30 ml) of oil, then fry the onion until golden. Add the turmeric and pepper and stir until fragrant. Mix in the mashed eggplants and cook, stirring, for 2 to 3 minutes. Push everything aside and make a large well in the center. Add a few tablespoons (30 ml) of oil to the well, then add the walnuts and garlic and cook until fragrant. Then add the dried mint and cook for about 30 seconds. Stir everything in the pan together. Add 5 tablespoons (75 ml) of water to loosen the paste, then cook over low heat with the lid on for 10 to 15 minutes.

Meanwhile, mix the kashk with ¼ cup (50 ml) of water. If you use goat cheese instead of kashk, combine the goat cheese with ¼ cup (65 ml) of water. Add the kashk to the pot and stir. Cook for 2 to 3 minutes, then serve.

Garnish with some fried crispy onions and crispy garlic if desired. Enjoy with a side of flatbread.

> ### NOTES
>
> Traditionally, this dish is made with eggplants fried in a pan until golden. The result is a creamy, caramelized eggplant, but to make this dish healthy, it's better to use the oven method.
>
> Kashk and cheese are both very salty. I recommend not adding salt to your dish until after you've added the cheese and tasted the dish.

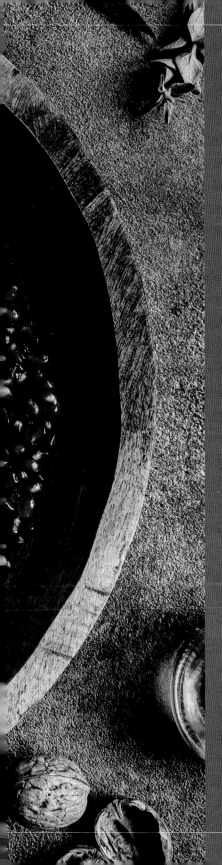

# Something to Appetize

No Persian table is complete without a few bowls of pickled vegetables, flavored yogurt dip or a small salad. These appetizing dishes are served in shared portions and are the final touches to unite the flavors of the meal. They are delightful garnishes that, unlike the other garnishes added by the chef, are presented in abundance to allow you to add as much as you desire.

Certain meals have perfect appetizer pairings that complement each other seamlessly. For instance, Green Beans and Beef Pilaf (page 57) goes well with Shirazi Salad (page 151) or Yogurt and Cucumber Dip (page 143). Additionally, fish dishes are often served with pickles.

These dips also make an excellent appetizer to go with chips or crackers.

# ROASTED EGGPLANT & YOGURT DIP

(Boraani Baademjaan/بورانی بادمجان)

*Boraani is a yogurt-based dip. There are wide varieties of boraani, and it is usually served as a side for main dishes or in big trays at parties as an appetizer with drinks. Boraani Baademjaan looks similar to baba ganoush in terms of look and texture, with eggplant being the common ingredient, but the taste and other ingredients differ. If you like smoky and garlicky dips, this dish is for you, although a non-smoky version is also widely popular. I explain how to make both kinds here.*

### SERVES 4-6

4 eggplants

Olive oil, as needed

Salt and pepper, to taste

2 cloves garlic, grated

2 cups (600 g) Greek yogurt

1 tsp smoked paprika, for garnish (optional)

1 tsp sesame seeds, for garnish (optional)

1 tbsp (4 g) finely chopped cilantro, for garnish (optional)

Roast the eggplants whole, skin on, on a charcoal grill until the inside is soft and the skin is charred. Leave them covered for 5 minutes, then peel the skin off and chop them finely.

Alternatively, make them in the oven or air fryer at 430°F (220°C) for 10 to 15 minutes. If using this method, you must char the skin with a kitchen torch to add the smoky flavor. Then cover and set aside for about 10 minutes, until the smoky flavor gets into the flesh. If you don't want them smokey, skip this step, peel the skin off and chop them finely.

Heat a few tablespoons (30 ml) of olive oil in a nonstick pan, then fry the mashed eggplants, stirring occasionally. Once the water evaporates and the eggplants have a pasty texture, add salt and pepper to taste, stir, then remove from the heat. Set the eggplants aside in a bowl until completely cooled down. Then add the garlic and yogurt to the eggplants and mix well.

You can serve the dip immediately or chill in the fridge until ready to serve. Garnish with smoked paprika, sesame seeds and cilantro if desired. Other garnishes that go well with this dish include ground cayenne red pepper, crispy shallots, a drizzle of olive oil or parsley.

# SPINACH & YOGURT DIP

(Boraani Esfenaaj/بورانی اسفناج)

*Here is another boraani made with spinach and garlic. It's an appetizer to serve at parties with drinks or as a side with a main dish. It's a healthy and flavor-packed recipe that's perfect for adding more spinach into your diet.*

## SERVES 4

Olive oil, as needed

14 oz (400 g) spinach

2 cloves garlic, grated

1½ cups (450 g) Greek or full-fat yogurt

1 tsp ground thyme

Salt and pepper, to taste

1 tsp rose petal powder, for garnish (optional)

1 tbsp (4 g) crispy shallot or Persian-Style Crispy Fried Onions (page 25), for garnish (optional)

1 tbsp (8 g) finely crushed walnuts, for garnish (optional)

2 tsp (1 g) dried mint, for garnish (optional)

In a large pot or pan with a lid over medium heat, add a few table-spoons (30 ml) of olive oil and let it heat up. Add the spinach, then cover with a lid and let the spinach wilt, stirring occasionally to avoid burning. Once the spinach is wilted and has shrunk, take the lid off and continue cooking until all the water evaporates and the spinach has a pasty texture. Try to break the spinach into smaller pieces with a spatula. Set the spinach aside in a bowl to cool down.

Stir the garlic and yogurt into the bowl with the spinach. Add the thyme, salt and pepper, and mix well.

You can serve the dip immediately or chill in the fridge until ready to serve. Garnish with the powdered rose petals, crispy shallot, walnuts and dried mint, if desired.

# YOGURT & CUCUMBER DIP

(Maast va Khiyaar/ماست و خیار)

*Persians love yogurt! We eat it in any shape: drinks, drained, drained and fermented, in stews and soups—you name it. Simple natural yogurt, or this yogurt dip, is served as a side with most meals. This dip makes a lovely appetizer accompanied by chips or crackers and alcoholic drinks.*

## SERVES 3–4

1 cup (150 g) finely chopped Persian cucumbers (see Note)

14 oz (400 g) Greek or full-fat yogurt

2 tsp (1 g) dried mint, plus more to garnish

½ tsp ground thyme

Salt and pepper, to taste

Dried rose petals, for garnish (optional)

Add the cucumbers, yogurt, dried mint, thyme, salt and pepper to a mixing bowl. Stir to combine.

Serve the dip in a serving bowl. Garnish with a sprinkle of dried mint and rose petals if desired.

> NOTE
>
> If you can only find regular long cucumbers, peel them, cut in half lengthwise, then scoop out the seeds before chopping.

# MARINATED OLIVES
# WITH HERBS, POMEGRANATE & WALNUTS
## (Zeytoon Parvardeh/زیتون پرورده)

*Zeytoon parvardeh is probably the most famous appetizer from Gilan province in northern Iran. In July 2023, TasteAtlas released a list of the ten best-rated vegetarian dishes in the world, and Zeytoon parvardeh took first place right above guacamole. In this recipe, the pomegranate is used in three ways: molasses, juice and arils—which takes olives to another level when paired with fragrant herbs and nutty walnut.*

### SERVES 4–6

1 cup (175 g) pomegranate arils, divided

3 tbsp (10 g) finely chopped cilantro

1 tbsp (5 g) finely chopped mint

1½ tbsp (5 g) finely chopped oregano leaves

2 tbsp (42 g) pomegranate molasses

3½ cups (100 g) walnuts

2–3 cloves garlic, chopped

6 tbsp (90 ml) juice of bitter oranges (see Notes)

3 tbsp (45 ml) olive oil

½ tsp Persian hogweed powder (optional, see Notes)

2⅓ cups (350 g) pitted green olives

Salt and pepper, to taste

Set aside ½ cup (75 g) of the pomegranate arils for garnish. In a blender, juice the remaining arils. Use a sieve to remove the seeds. Alternatively, you can use ¼ cup (60 ml) of ready-made pomegranate juice.

In a mixing bowl, combine the pomegranate juice with the cilantro, mint, oregano and pomegranate molasses.

In a food processor or using a mortar and pestle, grind the walnuts into a coarse paste, until the oil begins to release and the paste has a fine, coarse texture. Add the walnut paste along with the garlic, bitter-orange juice, olive oil and Persian hogweed (if using) to the mixing bowl. Mix everything well, then add the olives and give it a good stir. Taste, and add salt and pepper if needed.

Rest the olives in the fridge for up to 3 days, or serve right away. Garnish with the reserved pomegranate arils before serving.

### NOTES

Finding bitter oranges all year round can be tricky, but they have such an excellent acidic taste. I highly recommend using them if you can find them. As a substitute, mix 3 tablespoons (45 ml) of orange juice and 3 tablespoons (45 ml) of lemon juice plus the zest of half the lemon.

Persian hogweed is frequently used in Persian cuisine. It is hard to find in regular grocery stores in the Western world, but you can easily find them online or in Middle Eastern stores. It has a distinct aroma that can be overwhelming for those not used to it. However, if you are adventurous and curious to try new authentic flavors, I highly recommend using it; otherwise, it's totally fine to skip.

# QUICK PICKLED SMOKY EGGPLANT & HERBS

(Naaz Khaatoon/نازخاتون)

*A Persian table wouldn't be complete without a few small appetizer bowls here and there. We love pickles in many forms made with seasonal vegetables, and there is always a bowl of some torshi (what we call pickles in general) on our tables. Naaz Khaatoon is a quick pickle that originated from the north of Iran. It's one of my favorites not only because I don't need to wait weeks for it to be ready but also because it has verjuice (unripe grapes' juice) instead of vinegar, which makes it less sharp in taste and easier to eat in spoonfuls.*

### YIELDS 2 CUPS (450 G)

2 medium eggplants

2 tbsp (30 g) Mixed Herbs Chutney (page 26, see Notes)

1 green chile, finely chopped, or 1 tsp red chili flakes

½ cup (120 ml) verjuice

Pinch of salt

To cook the eggplants, grill them whole, skin on, on a charcoal grill. Cook until the inside is soft to the touch and the skin is charred. Using a grill to roast the eggplants is the preferred method as it creates the deep smoky flavor we are looking for in this recipe. For alternative methods, refer to the Notes.

Peel the eggplants and chop them finely, then mash with the back of your knife until soft. Add the eggplants, Mixed Herbs Chutney, chile, verjuice and a pinch of salt to a bowl and mix well. Let rest for 30 minutes in the fridge before serving.

Keep the pickled eggplants in a clean jar in the fridge; they should last for 7 to 10 days.

---

NOTES

Alternatively, cook the eggplants in the oven or an air fryer. Preheat the oven to 390°F (200°C). Lay the eggplants whole on a tray lined with parchment paper and cook under the grill until they are cooked through and have slightly charred skin, about 15 minutes. Be careful not to make the flesh dry.

Char the skin with a kitchen torch once the eggplants are cooked to give them a smoky flavor. Let them cool down, covered, for 10 to 15 minutes before peeling the skin.

To substitute for Mixed Herbs Chutney, finely chop ½ cup (25 g) of cilantro, 1 tablespoon (5 g) of mint and 1 tablespoon (5 g) of oregano until paste-like. Mix the herbs with ¼ teaspoon of salt.

---

# QUICK MANGO PICKLE
(Torshi Anbeh/ترشی انبه)

*This is a quick version of the beloved mango pickles from the southern provinces of Iran. The traditional long fermented pickle is made as a paste and is spicier. For this quick pickle, though, you can either mash the mango or use it chopped. It is a delicious sweet, spicy and acidic appetizer to accompany your dishes.*

## SERVES 8

1 large mango, peeled and cubed

1½ tbsp (27 g) salt

½ tbsp (5 g) ground turmeric

¼ cup (60 ml) white vinegar

¼ cup (60 ml) lime juice

½ tbsp (8 g) tomato paste

1 tbsp (8 g) tamarind paste without seeds

½ tsp mustard seeds

½ tsp coriander seeds

½ tsp red chili flakes

½ tsp fenugreek seeds

1 tsp nigella seeds

¼ tsp Persian hogweed powder

2–3 fresh or dried whole red chiles (optional)

1 tbsp (13 g) sugar

In a bowl, toss the mango with the salt and turmeric.

In a pot, bring 1 cup (240 ml) water to a boil, then add the vinegar, lime juice, tomato paste and tamarind paste and stir to combine.

In a pan, toast the mustard seeds, coriander seeds, chili flakes, fenugreek seeds, nigella seeds, Persian hogweed and red chiles, if using, together for 1 to 2 minutes, until fragrant. Add the toasted spices to the pot along with the mango and sugar and cook for 7 minutes.

Pour the pickle into an airtight glass container and let it cool down completely, uncovered. Then put the lid on tight and keep it in the fridge until ready to serve. Once chilled, you can serve immediately. You can keep the rest in the fridge for up to 2 to 3 weeks if there is no visual sign of spoilage.

# SHIRAZI SALAD

(سالاد شیرازی)

*I call this the controversial salad! It's a simple and delightful salad, but in the Middle East, each country has a slightly different version of it. Interestingly, the names usually carry a region in it—a way of showing ownership. I see it as how neighboring cultures and cuisines have influenced each other; the subtle differences are how they are separated. In Iran, this salad is known as Shirazi salad (coming from Shiraz, a city known internationally for its wine). Even in Iran, although Shirazi people are very particular about how they make this salad, there are a few established versions around the country, all called "Salad Shirazi." The traditional Shirazi recipe has no olive oil and is made with lots of verjuice to the point where it looks somewhat soupy and the ingredients are super finely chopped. The recipe here is how it is widely prepared in Tehran, where I grew up.*

## SERVES 4

8.8 oz (250 g) finely chopped Persian cucumbers (see Note)

1⅓ cups (250 g) tomatoes, seeds removed and finely chopped

⅓ cup (50 g) chopped red onion or the white part of green onions

⅓ cup (80 ml) verjuice or juice of 1 lime

1 tsp dried mint

Salt and pepper, to taste

1 tbsp (15 ml) olive oil (optional)

In a mixing bowl, combine the cucumbers, tomatoes, onion, verjuice, mint, salt, pepper and olive oil if using.

Serve the salad as a side with your meal.

> NOTE
>
> Persian cucumbers are small and crunchy and have a thin skin. They also have tiny seeds and are more flavorful. If you can find them in stores, use them for this salad; if not, though, regular cucumbers do fine. You'll need to peel them, cut them in half lengthwise and scoop the seeds out before chopping.

# Something Sweet

*The primary ingredients and flavors of Persian sweets include an assortment of nuts, spices such as cinnamon and cardamom—and warm and floral flavors like saffron and rose water. These flavors are delicately balanced, creating a subtle taste.*

*Fried dough stuffed with a mixture of nuts and spices and drenched in syrup or coated in powdered sugar can be found in various forms throughout different regions. Halva is another popular sweet that boasts diverse ingredients and flavors.*

*In this chapter, I will present you with various delectable options, including sweet bread, pastries, halva and more, all of which are sure to delight your senses.*

# MILK HALVA

(Halvaa-ye Shir/حلوای شیر)

---

*Halva is a beloved dessert made in many flavors in Iran. The Milk Halva has a soft texture—not as creamy as a pudding and not as rich and solid as a cake but something in between with sweet and gentle aromatic flavors. It is usually served in small portions with a cup of tea.*

---

SERVES 4–6

---

¾ cup (180 ml) whole milk

½ cup (110 g) sugar

⅛ tsp powdered saffron

3 tbsp (45 ml) rose water

½ cup (75 g) all-purpose flour

⅓ cup (80 ml) vegetable oil

⅓ cup (70 g) unsalted butter

½ cup (50 g) crushed toasted pistachios, for garnish

---

**NOTE**

There are many ways to serve halva, and you can get creative with it, but keep in mind that halva needs to still be warm when shaped; otherwise, it cracks.

---

Warm the milk with the sugar in a small saucepan and remove from the heat before it boils. Stir in the saffron and rose water. Let it sit warm over low heat and stir occasionally to avoid generating a skin on the top.

Sieve the flour into an 8- to 8½-inch (20- to 22-cm) nonstick pot with handles and start browning over medium-low heat until the flour turns into a light brown color, about 20 minutes. To toast the flour evenly and gradually without burning it, you should keep the temperature on medium-low and frequently stir it.

Once it has reached the desired color, sieve the flour again and put it back into the same pot, setting the heat on low. Add the vegetable oil and butter to the toasted flour and stir for 2 to 3 minutes.

Add the warm milk mixture to the flour in three to four steps, each time stirring fast with a wooden or rubber spatula for about 20 to 30 seconds. Continue until all the syrup is used and the halva has a soft texture like a smooth, thick paste.

Turn off the heat, grab your pot's handles and shake it left and right. This movement should bounce the halva in the pan side to side and make it come together as one big, soft lump. Once the halva comes together, it's ready to serve.

To serve, when it is still warm, you can pipe the halva into small paper cupcake liners for single portions or shape them in silicone mini-Bundt molds. If using silicone molds, let them cool down completely before removing them. You can also spread the halva when it's warm on a serving plate, flatten the surface with the back of a spoon and shape the edges like a pie as a sharing dessert. Once it is cooled down, you can cut it into small portions and serve. Garnish the halva with crushed pistachios right before serving.

To store, you can keep the halva in the same serving dish in the fridge, covered, for up to 5 days.

# GINGER HALVA

## (Halvaa-ye Zanjebil/حلوای زنجبیل)

*Halvaa-ye Zanjebil is a sweet dessert with aromas of ginger and cardamom that melts in the mouth. Ginger Halva is a traditional sweet from Tabriz city in the northwest of Iran, known for its delectable traditional food and dried fruits across the country. This halva goes well with a hot beverage.*

### YIELDS ABOUT 30 PIECES

1¾ cups (220 g) all-purpose flour

⅔ cup (145 g) butter

3 tbsp (45 ml) vegetable oil

1 cup (100 g) powdered sugar

1 tbsp (5 g) ground ginger, plus 1 tsp for extra spice

1 tsp ground cardamom

3 tbsp (24 g) ground pistachios or almonds

In a medium pot over medium heat, toast the flour until slightly colored, about 10 minutes, frequently stirring to toast the flour evenly.

Once the flour turns a bright beige color, add the butter and oil. Mix well until the butter melts. Cook for another couple of minutes, stirring often. Sieve the powdered sugar, ground ginger and ground cardamom and add them to the pot. Mix until well incorporated, then remove the pot from the heat.

Line an 8 x 8–inch (20 x 20–cm) square or 10 x 4–inch (25 x 10–cm) rectangular baking dish with parchment paper, then flatten the dough evenly on the bottom of the dish using the back of a spoon. Sprinkle the pistachios or almonds on top. Leave the baking dish in the freezer, uncovered, for about 30 minutes, until the halva hardens.

Cut the halva into small diamonds or square shapes (about 1 inch [2.5 cm]), then gently remove from the pan to serve. This halva has a crumbly texture, so you must be extra gentle when cutting and serving so as not to break them.

Alternatively, you can use a silicone mold to shape the halva into individual pieces. Make sure to freeze the mold for at least 1 hour before removing out the halva pieces.

# DEEP-FRIED MINI BUNS WITH NUTS & SPICES
## (Qottaab/قطاب)

*Qottaab is the traditional dessert of Yazd, the central province of Iran known for its historical architecture. Given the delectability of this dessert, it has turned into a beloved national sweet. I fondly remember my mom sitting us around to make little balls of qottaab together. I still can taste the warm fried dough, rolled in powdered sugar, unfolding in my mouth with flavors of nuts and spices; what a joy!*

### YIELDS ABOUT 28 PIECES

13½ tbsp (200 ml) water

⅓ cup (80 g) unsalted butter

2 cups (240 g) all-purpose flour

½ cup (60 g) walnuts

¼ cup (30 g) almonds

½ cup (50 g) powdered sugar, divided

¾ tsp ground cinnamon

¾ tsp ground cardamom

Cooking oil, as needed

In a medium pot, bring the water to a boil, then add the butter. Once the butter is melted, add the flour all at once. Turn the heat off and stir the flour until a soft dough forms. Set the dough aside to cool down.

Meanwhile, make the filling by grinding the walnuts and almonds together until a coarse powder forms. Add 2 tablespoons (16 g) of the powdered sugar, the cinnamon and cardamom powder to the nuts and mix well.

Once the dough is cooled down, roll it to about a 2 to 3–millimeter thickness. Cut out as many circles as possible from the dough using a 3-inch (7.5-cm) round cookie cutter. Fill each circle of dough with about 1 tablespoon (15 g) of the nut mixture, then bring the edges together and seal the dough. You can shape them into small balls or crescent forms.

In a small deep pot, add as much oil as needed to deep fry the pastries. They should be floating in the oil. Once the oil is hot, add the pastries to the oil a few at a time. Once golden on both sides, remove the pastries and leave them on a paper towel to absorb the excess oil.

After 10 minutes, roll each pastry in the remaining powdered sugar and serve.

> ### NOTE
> Alternatively, you can bake them in the oven. To do so, lay the pastries on a baking tray lined with parchment paper and bake them in the oven at 320°F (160°C) for about 15 minutes. They are ready once slightly colored on the edges. Take them out of the oven, let them cool down, then roll them in powdered sugar and serve.

# SESAME SWEET BREAD

## (Naan-e Komaaj/نان کماج)

*Naan-e komaaj is a popular bread for breakfast or with afternoon tea, especially during the fasting month. This version is from Hamadan, where their komaaj breads are the most famous. Komaaj is slightly sweet with a hint of rose water and cardamom. It has a somewhat dry texture, something between a scone and bread. It is supposed to be eaten with a hot beverage and goes well with butter or clotted cream.*

### YIELDS 6 BUNS

**SIMPLE SYRUP**

½ cup (100 g) sugar

⅓ cup (75 ml) water

1 tbsp (15 ml) rose water

½ tsp ground cardamom

**DOUGH**

½ cup (100 g) sugar

3½ oz (100 g) full-fat yogurt

1½ tbsp (25 ml) vegetable oil

1½ tbsp (25 ml) melted butter

1 tsp vanilla extract

2 tbsp (30 ml) rose water

¼ tsp salt

2¼ cups (275 g) all-purpose flour

1½ tsp (7 g) baking powder

1 egg yolk

2 tbsp (30 ml) milk

3 tbsp (27 g) white sesame seeds

Start by preparing the simple syrup. Mix the sugar, water and rose water in a pot with a thick bottom. Stir well until the sugar dissolves, then put it on high heat and let it come to a boil. After the syrup begins to boil, stop stirring. Let the syrup simmer for 2 to 3 minutes, until it thickens, then remove from the heat and set aside.

Preheat the oven to 356°F (180°C).

Prepare the dough by mixing the sugar, yogurt, oil and butter in a bowl. Add 3 tablespoons (45 ml) of the simple syrup, the vanilla, rose water and salt, and stir well. Sieve together the flour and baking powder and add them to the bowl. Mix all the ingredients well until the dough comes together. Do not knead the dough; just mix it enough to incorporate all the elements (the dough will be a bit sticky).

Line a baking tray with parchment paper. Dust your hands and your work surface with flour, then divide the dough into six pieces. Roll each piece loosely to shape it into a bun.

Place each bun on the tray at least 2 inches (5 cm) apart from each other. Using a cup or a bowl with a flat bottom, press each bun down into a ½-inch (1.3-cm)-thick disk. Use a cookie cutter smaller than the buns (any design you wish) and press it on each disk to create a pattern (do not press all the way down, just halfway). Beat the egg yolk with a fork, stir in the milk and brush the mixture over the buns. Sprinkle each bun with some sesame seeds.

Bake the buns in the middle rack of the oven for about 15 minutes, until they have risen and are golden. Meanwhile, add the cardamom to the remaining simple syrup. If the syrup is too thick, warm it briefly without stirring.

Immediately brush the warm buns with the cardamom syrup and let them cool down on a cooling rack before serving.

# DATE & NUTS MINI PIES
## (Kolompeh/کلمپه)

*Kolompeh is a traditional pie from Kerman province, one of the oldest civilizations in southeast Iran. The sweetness of these pies mainly comes from dates. They can be made with or without saffron so that you can adjust them to your liking. The spiced flavor of date filling makes these pies perfect for colder seasons.*

### YIELDS ABOUT 15 (3-INCH [7.5-CM]) PIES

## DOUGH

⅛ tsp powdered saffron (optional)

2 tbsp (30 ml) cooking oil or ghee

½ cup (120 g) unsalted butter, at room temperature

1 large egg

¼ tsp salt

½ cup (120 g) full-fat yogurt

2 tbsp (30 ml) rose water

3 tbsp (24 g) powdered sugar

2 cups (300 g) all-purpose flour

1 cup (100 g) chickpea or rice flour

2 tbsp (15 g) slivered pistachios, for garnish (optional)

## FILLING

2½ cups (200 g) pitted dates

7 tbsp (50 g) finely chopped walnuts

1 tbsp (6 g) freshly ground cardamom

1 tsp cinnamon

½ tsp ground ginger

1 tbsp (15 ml) rose water

If using saffron, add it to a ramekin with 3 tablespoons (45 ml) of cold water and set aside.

Cream together the oil and butter until fluffy and white. Add the egg and mix until incorporated. Then add the brewed saffron (if using), salt, yogurt and rose water and mix well. Sieve the powdered sugar and both flours into the bowl. Gently, with the tip of your fingers, form the dough. Mix until the dough is soft and even, but avoid kneading. Cover the dough in plastic wrap and rest in the fridge for 2 hours.

Preheat the oven to 320°F (160°C).

Prepare the filling. If your dates are hard, let them soak with ¼ cup (60 ml) of hot water for about 10 minutes, until they soften. When the dates are ready, blend them in a food processor until soft and pasty. In a bowl, mix the dates, walnuts, cardamom, cinnamon, ginger and rose water.

Line a baking tray with parchment paper. Dust your hands and your work surface with flour. Flatten the dough with a rolling pin to about ½-centimeter thickness. Cut out as many circles as possible from the dough using a 3-inch (7.5-cm) round cookie cutter. Put 1 teaspoon of the date filling in the center of half of the dough circles. Cover each filled circle with an unfilled circle of dough (like a ravioli). Gently press the edges to seal, then using a cookie stamp, press down the center with the filling until flat. Seal the edges by pressing with a fork or wrapping inward, then lay on the baking sheet. Repeat until all the dough is used.

Garnish the mini pies with some crushed slivered pistachios (if using). Bake on the middle rack for about 15 minutes, until the edges are slightly colored. Let the mini pies cool down on a cooling rack before serving.

# RICE VERMICELLI & ROSE WATER GRANITA
## (Faaloodeh/فالوده)

*Faaloodeh is a beloved summer dessert, much like granita in terms of preparation and texture, with one difference—rice noodles, which add an extra layer of texture and interest to this traditional dessert. The icy part is fragrant with rose water and lime juice, topped with the sweetness of berry syrup. It is a perfect dessert to fight the heat. The city of Shiraz, besides its known wine, is famous for its faaloodeh.*

### SERVES 4

1 cup (200 g) sugar

¼ cup (60 ml) rose water

2.1 oz (60 g) rice vermicelli

Juice of 2 limes

4 tbsp (80 g) berry jam or syrup, for garnish

In a small saucepan, bring 2½ cups (600 ml) water and the sugar to a boil. Cook and stir until the sugar is dissolved, then add the rose water and remove from the heat. Transfer to an 8-inch (20-cm) square dish and cool to room temperature.

Meanwhile, cook the noodles, cut them into small pieces using kitchen scissors and keep them in a bowl with cold water.

Freeze the syrup for 1 hour, then take it out and stir with a fork. Add the noodles, then freeze for another 2 hours, stirring every 30 minutes. Keep in the freezer until completely frozen.

Stir the granita with a fork before serving, then spoon into dessert dishes. Garnish with lime juice and berry syrup.

# SAFFRON & CARDAMOM BUNS

## (Naan-e Shirmaal Zaferaani/نان شیرمال زعفرانی)

*Fluffy, sweet and with a hint of cardamom, this bread is widely consumed all over Iran. It's perfect for breakfast or to enjoy with a hot cup of tea in the afternoon. Naan-e shirmaal has two versions, one with saffron and one without, so skip the saffron if you wish.*

### YIELDS 4 BUNS

2½ tsp (10 g) active dry yeast

⅛ tsp powdered saffron (optional)

½ cup (120 ml) whole milk, at room temperature

½ cup (120 ml) cooking oil

1 egg, at room temperature

⅔ cup (120 g) sugar

½ tsp cardamom

3¾ cups (480 g) all-purpose flour, plus more as needed

1 egg yolk, for brushing

1 tbsp (15 ml) milk, for brushing

1 tbsp (15 ml) cooking oil, for brushing

2 tbsp (18 g) sesame seeds (white or black or both)

Mix the yeast and saffron (if using) in ½ cup (120 ml) lukewarm water and let sit for 5 to 10 minutes, until foamy. Add the milk, oil, egg, sugar and cardamom and mix well. Stir in half of the flour and mix, then add the rest. Mix well until a dough forms. The dough should be sticky, but add a few more tablespoons (28 g) of flour if it feels too sticky. Cover the bowl and rest in a warm place for about 1½ hours until it doubles in size.

Preheat the oven to 355°F (180°C). In a small bowl, mix the egg yolk with the milk and oil.

Dust your hands and work surface with flour. Shape the dough into a ball. Cut the dough into four equal pieces, then form each piece into a ball.

Line a baking dish with parchment paper. Dust with flour, then arrange the buns, leaving 3 to 4 inches (7.5 to 10 cm) between them. Flatten each bun with your hand, then create dents with the tip of your fingers. You can oil your fingers to make it easier. Brush the buns with the egg yolk mixture, then sprinkle with sesame seeds. Bake in the oven for 15 to 20 minutes, until they are fluffy and the tops are golden brown.

Move the buns to a cooling rack and cover with a kitchen towel for the first 10 minutes, then remove the towel and cool completely before serving.

> ### NOTE
> You can cut the dough into eight pieces to make smaller buns, or cut it into three long pieces and braid it to have one larger braided dough.

# ACKNOWLEDGMENTS

I would like to express my gratitude for the incredible support I received throughout the process of bringing this book to life. It is a privilege to share my love for cooking with food enthusiasts and see the joy my recipes bring to their tables.

I am incredibly grateful to my husband for his unwavering belief in my abilities. He was always by my side to shine a light on my path whenever the road got dark and wavy. His feedback has been invaluable, as he has always been my toughest critic. He was the one testing each recipe firsthand.

I extend my heartfelt thanks to Page Street Publishing and my fantastic editors, Emily Archbold, Aïcha Martine Thiam and Marissa Giambelluca. They believed in my work and went above and beyond to make this book come to life the way I dreamed of it.

I want to express my gratitude to my amazing agent, Felice Laverne, for providing me with tireless assistance every step of the way.

I also want to mention the invaluable support of my friends and colleagues who cheered for me, gave me constructive feedback and generously shared their experiences and knowledge with me. Stephanie Well-Sarcina, Michal Narozny, Jeb Inge and Leandro Silva: I want to thank you all for your support along the way.

Finally, I would like to thank my community of food enthusiasts on Instagram. Their support and friendship have been invaluable to me throughout the last five years. I have learned and refined my skills alongside them; this book wouldn't have been possible without their support.

# ABOUT THE AUTHOR

**Haniyeh Nikoo** is a recipe developer, food stylist and photographer. While studying graphic design in Iran, she began to develop her passion for photography. She further pursued photography as a visual arts graduate student in Strasbourg, France. She relied on these experiences as a solid base when her love for cooking shifted her focus to food photography and styling.

Haniyeh's exceptional culinary creations showcase her profound admiration for the gastronomic arts. Her remarkable photography skills capture the essence and beauty of food, elevating both the visual and culinary experience for the viewer.

# INDEX

## A

almonds
  Deep-Fried Mini Buns with Nuts & Spices, 159
  Ginger Halva, 156
  Rainbow Rice with Lamb, 49–50

## B

barberries
  Carrot Rice with Chicken Thighs, 63–64
  overview, 14
  Rainbow Rice with Lamb, 49–50
  Saffron, Yogurt & Chicken Rice Pilaf, 67–68
  Tabrizi Stuffed Eggplant, 131
barley: Barley & Cilantro Soup, 100
Bean & Tomato Stew
  recipe, 96
  Tomato Paste Omelet with Beans, 112
beef
  Green Beans & Beef Pilaf, 57–58
  Ground Beef Kabaab, 31
  Lentil Rice with Raisins & Ground Beef, 61–62
  Meatballs in Mint & Vinegar Sauce, 91
  Meat & Potato Patties, 128
  Sweet & Sour Kabaab, 35
  Tabrizi Stuffed Eggplant, 131
berry jam: Rice Vermicelli & Rose Water Granita, 164
borlotti beans: Herby Bean Stew with Smoked Fish, 75
broad beans: Broad Bean & Dill Pilaf, 71
buttermilk
  Barley & Cilantro Soup, 100

Buttermilk, Walnut & Tomato Soup, 95
buttermilk paste
  Buttermilk, Walnut & Tomato Soup, 95
  Eggplant & Buttermilk Spread, 135
  overview, 13–14
butternut squash
  Butternut Squash Patties, 107
  Walnut, Pumpkin & Pomegranate Stew, 76

## C

carrots
  Barley & Cilantro Soup, 100
  Carrot Rice with Chicken Thighs, 63–64
celery
  Carrot Rice with Chicken Thighs, 63–64
  Celery & Lamb Stew, 79
chicken
  Carrot Rice with Chicken Thighs, 63–64
  Chicken in Pomegranate Sauce, 87
  Chicken Kabaab, 32
  Saffron, Yogurt & Chicken Rice Pilaf, 67–68
chickpea flour
  Date & Nuts Mini Pies, 163
  Meatballs in Mint & Vinegar Sauce, 91
chickpeas: Lamb & Beans Stew, 88
cranberries
  as barberry substitute, 14
  Tabrizi Stuffed Eggplant, 131
cucumbers
  Cold Yogurt Soup with Fresh Herbs & Nuts, 103
  Shirazi Salad, 151

Yogurt & Cucumber Dip, 143
curry
  Bean & Tomato Stew, 96
  Carrot Rice with Chicken Thighs, 63–64
  Saffron, Yogurt & Chicken Rice Pilaf, 67–68
  Spicy Red Lentil Daal, 99
  Spicy Shrimp & Potatoes, 124
  Spicy Shrimp Rice with Tamarind, 55–56
  Stuffed Fish, 36
  Tabrizi Stuffed Eggplant, 131
  Tamarind Spicy Fish Stew, 83

## D

Dallaar
  Quick Pickled Smoky Eggplant & Herbs, 147
  recipe, 26
dates
  Date & Nuts Mini Pies, 163
  Date, Walnut & Sesame Omelet, 115
  Mung Bean, Tahini & Date Rice, 51–52

## E

eggplants
  Eggplant & Buttermilk Spread, 135
  Eggplant, Lamb & Tomato Stew, 80
  Quick Pickled Smoky Eggplant & Herbs, 147
  Roasted Eggplant & Yogurt Dip, 139
  Smoky Eggplant & Tomato Spread, 132
  Smoky Eggplant & Walnut Dip, 127
  Tabrizi Stuffed Eggplant, 131

eggs
 Butternut Squash Patties, 107
 Date & Nuts Mini Pies, 163
 Date, Walnut & Sesame
  Omelet, 115
 Fried Cheese Omelet, 111
 Herby Bean Stew with
  Smoked Fish, 75
 Lettuce & Dill Patties, 123
 Meat & Potato Patties, 128
 Saffron & Cardamom Buns, 167
 Saffron, Yogurt & Chicken
  Rice Pilaf, 67–68
 Sesame Sweet Bread, 160
 Smoky Eggplant & Tomato
  Spread, 132
 Spinach Onion Omelet, 108
 Tomato Paste Omelet with
  Beans, 112

F
feta cheese
 Fried Cheese Omelet, 111
 Meat & Potato Patties, 128
fish
 Herby Bean Stew with
  Smoked Fish, 75
 Stuffed Fish, 36
 Tamarind Spicy Fish Stew, 83

G
garlic
 Barley & Cilantro Soup, 100
 Bean & Tomato Stew, 96
 Chicken in Pomegranate
  Sauce, 87
 Eggplant & Buttermilk
  Spread, 135
 Fried Cheese Omelet, 111
 Herby Bean Stew with
  Smoked Fish, 75
 Marinated Olives with Herbs,
  Pomegranate & Walnuts,
  144

Roasted Eggplant & Yogurt
 Dip, 139
Smoky Eggplant & Tomato
 Spread, 132
Smoky Eggplant & Walnut
 Dip, 127
Spicy Red Lentil Daal, 99
Spicy Shrimp & Potatoes, 124
Spicy Shrimp Rice with
 Tamarind, 55–56
Spinach Onion Omelet, 108
Spinach & Yogurt Dip, 140
Stuffed Fish, 36
Tabrizi Stuffed Eggplant, 131
ginger
 Date & Nuts Mini Pies, 163
 Ginger Halva, 156
 Rice Mixed Spices, 21
goat cheese
 Buttermilk, Walnut & Tomato
  Soup, 95
 Eggplant & Buttermilk
  Spread, 135
grapes
 Eggplant, Lamb & Tomato
  Stew, 80
 overview, 17
green beans: Green Beans &
 Beef Pilaf, 57–58

H
harissa powder: Spicy Shrimp &
 Potatoes, 124
hogweed
 Bean & Tomato Stew, 96
 Marinated Olives with Herbs,
  Pomegranate & Walnuts,
  144
 overview, 16–17
 Quick Mango Pickle, 148
 Tomato Paste Omelet with
  Beans, 112

Walnut, Pumpkin & Pome-
 granate Stew, 76
honey: Clotted Cream, 116

K
kashk
 Buttermilk, Walnut & Tomato
  Soup, 95
 Eggplant & Buttermilk
  Spread, 135
 overview, 13–14

L
lamb
 Braised Lamb Shank, 84
 Celery & Lamb Stew, 79
 Eggplant, Lamb & Tomato
  Stew, 80
 Ground Beef Kabaab, 31
 Lamb & Beans Stew, 88
 Rainbow Rice with Lamb,
  49–50
 Sweet & Sour Kabaab, 35
lemons
 Bean & Tomato Stew, 96
 Celery & Lamb Stew, 79
 Chicken Kabaab, 32
 Spinach Onion Omelet, 108
 Tomato Paste Omelet with
  Beans, 112
lentils
 Lentil Rice with Raisins &
  Ground Beef, 61–62
 Spicy Red Lentil Daal, 99
lettuce: Lettuce & Dill Patties,
 123
limes
 dried, 14
 Quick Mango Pickle, 148
 Rice Vermicelli & Rose Water
  Granita, 164
 Shirazi Salad, 151
 Spicy Shrimp & Potatoes, 124

Stuffed Fish, 36
Sweet & Sour Kabaab, 35

M

mangoes: Quick Mango Pickle, 148
Mixed Herbs Chutney
  Quick Pickled Smoky Eggplant & Herbs, 147
  recipe, 26
Mixed Rice Spices
  Green Beans & Beef Pilaf, 57–58
  Mung Bean, Tahini & Date Rice, 51–52
mung beans: Mung Bean, Tahini & Date Rice, 51–52
mutton: Lamb & Beans Stew, 88

N

nigella seeds: Quick Mango Pickle, 148

O

oats: Barley & Cilantro Soup, 100
olives: Marinated Olives with Herbs, Pomegranate & Walnuts, 144
onions
  Barley & Cilantro Soup, 100
  Bean & Tomato Stew, 96
  Braised Lamb Shank, 84
  Buttermilk, Walnut & Tomato Soup, 95
  Celery & Lamb Stew, 79
  Chicken in Pomegranate Sauce, 87
  Chicken Kabaab, 32
  Cold Yogurt Soup with Fresh Herbs & Nuts, 103
  Eggplant & Buttermilk Spread, 135
  Eggplant, Lamb & Tomato Stew, 80

Green Beans & Beef Pilaf, 57–58
Ground Beef Kabaab, 31
Lamb & Beans Stew, 88
Lentil Rice with Raisins & Ground Beef, 61–62
Meatballs in Mint & Vinegar Sauce, 91
Meat & Potato Patties, 128
Mung Bean, Tahini & Date Rice, 51–52
Persian-Style Crispy Fried Onions, 25
Rainbow Rice with Lamb, 49–50
Saffron, Yogurt & Chicken Rice Pilaf, 67–68
Shirazi Salad, 151
Spicy Red Lentil Daal, 99
Spicy Shrimp & Potatoes, 124
Spicy Shrimp Rice with Tamarind, 55–56
Spinach & Yogurt Dip, 140
Spinach Onion Omelet, 108
Stuffed Fish, 36
Sweet & Sour Kabaab, 35
Tabrizi Stuffed Eggplant, 131
Tamarind Spicy Fish Stew, 83
Walnut, Pumpkin & Pomegranate Stew, 76
orange
  Bean & Tomato Stew, 96
  Marinated Olives with Herbs, Pomegranate & Walnuts, 144
  Rainbow Rice with Lamb, 49–50
  Spinach Onion Omelet, 108
  Tomato Paste Omelet with Beans, 112

P

Persian hogweed
  Bean & Tomato Stew, 96

Marinated Olives with Herbs, Pomegranate & Walnuts, 144
overview, 16–17
Quick Mango Pickle, 148
Tomato Paste Omelet with Beans, 112
Walnut, Pumpkin & Pomegranate Stew, 76
Persian Plain Rice
  Bread & Saffron Crispy Bottom, 45
  Celery & Lamb Stew, 79
  Chelo with Yogurt & Saffron Crispy Rice, 42
  Chicken in Pomegranate Sauce, 87
  Crispy Potato Bottom of the Pot, 46
  Eggplant, Lamb & Tomato Stew, 80
  Rainbow Rice with Lamb, 49–50
  Tamarind Spicy Fish Stew, 83
Persian-Style Crispy Fried Onions
  Barley & Cilantro Soup, 100
  Buttermilk, Walnut & Tomato Soup, 95
  Eggplant & Buttermilk Spread, 135
  Lentil Rice with Raisins & Ground Beef, 61–62
  Meatballs in Mint & Vinegar Sauce, 91
  Spinach & Yogurt Dip, 140
pinto beans: Bean & Tomato Stew, 96
pistachios
  Carrot Rice with Chicken Thighs, 63–64
  Date & Nuts Mini Pies, 163
  Ginger Halva, 156
  Milk Halva, 155
  Rainbow Rice with Lamb, 49–50

Saffron, Yogurt & Chicken Rice Pilaf, 67–68

pomegranate arils

Chicken in Pomegranate Sauce, 87

Marinated Olives with Herbs, Pomegranate & Walnuts, 144

Smoky Eggplant & Walnut Dip, 127

Stuffed Fish, 36

Walnut, Pumpkin & Pomegranate Stew, 76

pomegranate molasses

Chicken in Pomegranate Sauce, 87

Marinated Olives with Herbs, Pomegranate & Walnuts, 144

Smoky Eggplant & Walnut Dip, 127

Stuffed Fish, 36

Sweet & Sour Kabaab, 35

Walnut, Pumpkin & Pomegranate Stew, 76

potatoes

Bean & Tomato Stew, 96

Carrot Rice with Chicken Thighs, 63–64

Crispy Potato Bottom of the Pot, 46

Green Beans & Beef Pilaf, 57–58

Lamb & Beans Stew, 88

Meat & Potato Patties, 128

Spicy Red Lentil Daal, 99

Spicy Shrimp & Potatoes, 124

pumpkin: Walnut, Pumpkin & Pomegranate Stew, 76

Q

quinces: Quince Jam, 119

R

radishes: Cold Yogurt Soup with Fresh Herbs & Nuts, 103

raisins

Cold Yogurt Soup with Fresh Herbs & Nuts, 103

Lentil Rice with Raisins & Ground Beef, 61–62

rice

Braised Lamb Shank, 84

Bread & Saffron Crispy Bottom, 45

Broad Bean & Dill Pilaf, 71

Carrot Rice with Chicken Thighs, 63–64

Celery & Lamb Stew, 79

Chelo with Yogurt & Saffron Crispy Rice, 42

Chicken in Pomegranate Sauce, 87

Chicken Kabaab, 32

Crispy Potato Bottom of the Pot, 46

Eggplant, Lamb & Tomato Stew, 80

Green Beans & Beef Pilaf, 57–58

Ground Beef Kabaab, 31

Herby Bean Stew with Smoked Fish, 75

Lentil Rice with Raisins & Ground Beef, 61–62

Meatballs in Mint & Vinegar Sauce, 91

Mung Bean, Tahini & Date Rice, 51–52

overview, 13

Persian Plain Rice, 41

Rainbow Rice with Lamb, 49–50

Saffron, Yogurt & Chicken Rice Pilaf, 67–68

Spicy Shrimp & Potatoes, 124

Spicy Shrimp Rice with Tamarind, 55–56

Sweet & Sour Kabaab, 35

Tamarind Spicy Fish Stew, 83

Walnut, Pumpkin & Pomegranate Stew, 76

rice flour: Date & Nuts Mini Pies, 163

Rice Mixed Spices

Carrot Rice with Chicken Thighs, 63–64

Green Beans & Beef Pilaf, 57–58

Lentil Rice with Raisins & Ground Beef, 61–62

Mung Bean, Tahini & Date Rice, 51–52

recipe, 21

rice vermicelli: Rice Vermicelli & Rose Water Granita, 164

S

saffron

Braised Lamb Shank, 84

Bread & Saffron Crispy Bottom, 45

Chelo with Yogurt & Saffron Crispy Rice, 42

Chicken Kabaab, 32

Crispy Potato Bottom of the Pot, 46

Date & Nuts Mini Pies, 163

Green Beans & Beef Pilaf, 57–58

Ground Beef Kabaab, 31

Lentil Rice with Raisins & Ground Beef, 61–62

Milk Halva, 155

overview, 16

Rainbow Rice with Lamb, 49–50

Saffron & Cardamom Buns, 167

Saffron, Yogurt & Chicken Rice Pilaf, 67–68

Spicy Shrimp Rice with Tamarind, 55–56

Spinach Onion Omelet, 108

sesame seeds

Date, Walnut & Sesame Omelet, 115

Mung Bean, Tahini & Date
  Rice, 51–52
Roasted Eggplant & Yogurt
  Dip, 139
Saffron & Cardamom Buns,
  167
Sesame Sweet Bread, 160
shallots: Spinach & Yogurt Dip,
  140
shrimp
  Spicy Shrimp & Potatoes, 124
  Spicy Shrimp Rice with
    Tamarind, 55–56
spinach
  Spinach Onion Omelet, 108
  Spinach & Yogurt Dip, 140
squash
  Butternut Squash Patties, 107
  Walnut, Pumpkin & Pome-
    granate Stew, 76
Stew Mixed Spices
  Eggplant, Lamb & Tomato
    Stew, 80
  Lentil Rice with Raisins &
    Ground Beef, 61–62
  recipe, 22

T
tahini: Mung Bean, Tahini &
  Date Rice, 51–52
tamarind paste
  Quick Mango Pickle, 148
  Spicy Red Lentil Daal, 99
  Spicy Shrimp Rice with
    Tamarind, 55–56
  Tamarind Spicy Fish Stew, 83
tamarind pulp: Spicy Red Lentil
  Daal, 99
tomatoes
  Bean & Tomato Stew, 96
  Buttermilk, Walnut & Tomato
    Soup, 95
  Chicken Kabaab, 32
  Eggplant, Lamb & Tomato
    Stew, 80
  Ground Beef Kabaab, 31

Lamb & Beans Stew, 88
Lettuce & Dill Patties, 123
Shirazi Salad, 151
Smoky Eggplant & Tomato
  Spread, 132
Sweet & Sour Kabaab, 35
Tabrizi Stuffed Eggplant, 131
tomato paste
  Bean & Tomato Stew, 96
  Chicken in Pomegranate
    Sauce, 87
  Eggplant, Lamb & Tomato
    Stew, 80
  Green Beans & Beef Pilaf,
    57–58
  Lamb & Beans Stew, 88
  Quick Mango Pickle, 148
  Rainbow Rice with Lamb,
    49–50
  Smoky Eggplant & Tomato
    Spread, 132
  Spicy Shrimp & Potatoes, 124
  Tabrizi Stuffed Eggplant, 131
  Tamarind Spicy Fish Stew, 83
  Tomato Paste Omelet with
    Beans, 112
turnips: Herby Bean Stew with
  Smoked Fish, 75

V
verjuice
  Quick Pickled Smoky
    Eggplant & Herbs, 147
  Shirazi Salad, 151

W
walnuts
  Buttermilk, Walnut & Tomato
    Soup, 95
  Cold Yogurt Soup with Fresh
    Herbs & Nuts, 103
  Date & Nuts Mini Pies, 163
  Date, Walnut & Sesame
    Omelet, 115
  Deep-Fried Mini Buns with
    Nuts & Spices, 159

Eggplant & Buttermilk
  Spread, 135
Marinated Olives with Herbs,
  Pomegranate & Walnuts,
  144
Smoky Eggplant & Walnut
  Dip, 127
Spinach & Yogurt Dip, 140
Stuffed Fish, 36
Sweet & Sour Kabaab, 35
Walnut, Pumpkin & Pome-
  granate Stew, 76
white beans
  Bean & Tomato Stew, 96
  Lamb & Beans Stew, 88

Y
yeast: Saffron & Cardamom
  Buns, 167
yogurt
  Barley & Cilantro Soup, 100
  Chelo with Yogurt & Saffron
    Crispy Rice, 42
  Cold Yogurt Soup with Fresh
    Herbs & Nuts, 103
  Date & Nuts Mini Pies, 163
  Meatballs in Mint & Vinegar
    Sauce, 91
  Roasted Eggplant & Yogurt
    Dip, 139
  Saffron, Yogurt & Chicken
    Rice Pilaf, 67–68
  Sesame Sweet Bread, 160
  Spinach & Yogurt Dip, 140
  Yogurt & Cucumber Dip, 143